ACADEMICS, DISCIPLINE, AND SPORTS AT SAINT FINBARR'S COLLEGE

ACADEMICS, DISCIPLINE, AND SPORTS AT SAINT FINBARR'S COLLEGE

Tributes to Finbarr's Great Soccer Players

Deji Badiru

Academics, Discipline, and Sports at Saint Finbarr's College
Tributes to Finbarr's Great Soccer Players

iUniverse books may be ordered through booksellers or by contacting:

iUniverse
1663 Liberty Drive
Bloomington, IN 47403
www.iuniverse.com
844-349-9409

ISBN: 978-1-6632-4983-8 (sc)
ISBN: 978-1-6632-4984-5 (e)

Library of Congress Control Number: 2023900678

Print information available on the last page.

iUniverse rev. date: 01/16/2023

CONTENTS

Books in the ABICS Publications Book Series
(www.abicspublications.com)

1. **Academics, Discipline, and Sports at Saint Finbarr's College: Tributes to Finbarr's Great Soccer Players**, 2023
2. **More Physics of Soccer: Playing the Game Smart and Safe**, 2022
3. **Rapidity: Time Management on the Dot**, iUniverse, Bloomington, Indiana, 2022.
4. **The Physics of Skateboarding: Fun, Fellowship, and Following**, 2021.
5. **My Everlasting Education at Saint Finbarr's College: Academics, Discipline, and Sports**, 2020.
6. **Twenty-Fifth Hour: Secrets to Getting More Done Every Day**, 2020.
7. **Kitchen Project Management: The Art and Science of an Organized Kitchen**, 2020.
8. **Wives of the Same School: Tributes and Straight Talk**, 2019
9. **The Rooster and the Hen: The Story of Love at Last Look**, 2018
10. **Kitchen Physics: Dynamic Nigerian Recipes**, 2018.
11. *The Story of Saint Finbarr's College: Father Slattery's Contributions to Education and Sports in Nigeria,* 2018.
12. **Physics of Soccer II: Science and Strategies for a Better Game**, 2018
13. **Kitchen Dynamics: The rice way**, 2015
14. **Consumer Economics: The value of dollars and sense for money management**, 2015
15. **Youth Soccer Training Slides: A Math and Science Approach**, 2014
16. **My Little Blue Book of Project Management**, 2014
17. **8 by 3 Paradigm for Time Management**, 2013
18. **Badiru's Equation of Student Success: Intelligence, Common Sense, and Self-discipline**, 2013
19. **Isi Cookbook: Collection of Easy Nigerian Recipes**, 2013

ABICS Publications
A Division of
AB International Consulting Services

ABICS PUBLICATIONS
Books for Home,
Work, & Leisure

AUTHOR'S EXTENDED BIOGRAPHICAL SKETCH

Professor Adedeji Badiru (Deji Badiru) is a Professor of Systems Engineering and also SES-level Dean of the Graduate School of Engineering and Management at the Air Force Institute of Technology (AFIT). He has oversight for planning, directing, and controlling operations related to granting doctoral and master's degrees for the US Air Force. He was previously Professor and Head of Systems Engineering and Management at AFIT, Professor and Department Head of Industrial Engineering at the University of Tennessee - Knoxville, and Professor of Industrial Engineering and Dean of University College at the University of Oklahoma, Norman. He is a registered Professional Engineer (PE), a certified Project Management Professional (PMP), a Fellow of the Institute of Industrial & Systems Engineers, a Fellow of the Industrial Engineering and Operations Management Society, and a Fellow of the Nigerian Academy of Engineering. He is also a Program Evaluator for ABET. He holds a leadership certificate from the University Tennessee Leadership Institute. He has BS in Industrial Engineering, MS in Mathematics, and MS in Industrial Engineering from Tennessee Technological University, and Ph.D. in Industrial Engineering from the University of Central Florida. His areas of interest include mathematical modeling, project modeling and analysis, economic analysis, systems engineering modeling, computer simulation, and productivity analysis. He is a prolific author, with over 38 books, over 32 book chapters, over 140 Journal and magazine articles, and over 200 conference presentations. He is a member of several professional associations and scholastic honor societies. Professor Badiru, a world-renowned educator, has won several awards for his teaching, research, administrative, and professional accomplishments. Some of his selected awards include the 2009 Dayton Affiliate Society Council Award for Outstanding Scientists and Engineers in the Education category with a commendation from the 128th Senate of Ohio, 2010 ASEE John Imhoff Award for his global contributions to Industrial Engineering Education, the 2011 Federal Employee of the Year Award in the Managerial Category from the International Public Management Association, Wright Patterson Air Force Base, the 2012 Distinguished Engineering Alum Award from the University of Central Florida, the 2012 Medallion Award from the Institute of Industrial Engineers for his global contributions in the advancement of the profession, 2016 Outstanding Global Engineering Education Award from the Industrial Engineering and Operations Management, 2015 Air Force-level Winner of the National Public Service Award from The American Society for Public Administration and the National Academy of Public Administration, 2013 Father D. J. Slattery Excellence Award from Saint Finbarr's College Alumni Association - North America, 2013 Award Team Leader, Air Force Organizational Excellence Award for Air University C3 (Cost Conscious Culture), 2013 Finalist for Jefferson Science Fellows Program, National Academy of Sciences, 2012 Book-of-the-Month Recognition for Statistical Techniques for Project Control from the Industrial Engineering Magazine, the 2009 Industrial Engineering Joint Publishers Book-of-the-Year Award for The Handbook of Military Industrial Engineering and 2020 for The Story of Industrial Engineering. Professor Badiru is also the book series editor for CRC Press/Taylor & Francis book series on Systems Innovation. He has served as a consultant to several organizations around the world including Russia, UK, Canada, Mexico, Taiwan, Nigeria, and Ghana. He has conducted customized training workshops for numerous organizations including

Sony, AT&T, Seagate Technology, U.S. Air Force, Oklahoma Gas & Electric, Oklahoma Asphalt Pavement Association, Hitachi, Nigeria National Petroleum Corporation, and ExxonMobil. He has served as a Technical Project Reviewer, curriculum reviewer, and proposal reviewer for several organizations including The Third-World Network of Scientific Organizations, Italy, Social Sciences and Humanities Research Council of Canada, National Science Foundation, National Research Council, and the American Council on Education. He is on the editorial and review boards of several technical journals and book publishers. Prof. Badiru has also served as an Industrial Development Consultant to the United Nations Development Program. In 2011, Prof. Badiru led a research team to develop analytical models for Systems Engineering Research Efficiency (SEER) for the Air Force acquisitions integration office at the Pentagon. He has led a multi-year multi-million-dollar research collaboration between the Air Force Institute of Technology and KBR Aerospace Group. Prof. Badiru has diverse areas of avocation. His professional accomplishments are coupled with his passion for writing about everyday events and interpersonal issues, especially those dealing with social responsibility. Outside of the academic realm, he writes motivational poems, editorials, and newspaper commentaries; as well as engaging in paintings and crafts. Professor Badiru is the 2020 recipient of the Lifetime Achievement Award from Taylor and Francis publishing group. He was also part of the AFIT team that led the institution's receipt of the 2019/2020 US Air Force Organizational Excellence Award. Professor Badiru is also the recipient of the 2022 BEYA career achievement award in Government category. He holds a US Trademark for DEJI Systems Model for Design, Evaluation, Justification, and Integration.

DEDICATION

Dedicated to the memory of **Reverend Father Denis J. Slattery** (February 29, 1916 – July 7, 2003, an Irish Catholic Priest, who invested his entire clergy career to Saint Finbarr's College and the advancement of sports in Nigeria. May his soul rest in peace.

Also recognized in this dedication is **Pelé** (born Edson Arantes do Nascimento: October 23, 1940 – December 29, 2022), the soccer legend, who transformed the game of soccer into a worldwide phenomenon, adoringly referred to as the "beautiful game." Beyond his soccer field skills, he was the ultimate soccer gentleman and ambassador. May his soul rest in peace.

STATEMENT OF ENDORSEMENT

Nothing tells the story of a book better than an endorsement from someone of high regard, who is very close to the theme and premise of the book. Below is the statement of endorsement by former Soccer Great of Saint Finbarr's College, Mr. Paul Okoku.

==================================

"The stories, accounts, testimonies, graphics, and pictures in this book help solidify the book's overall goal, content, and quality for the readers. Particularly, the chapter dedicated to my content production. I thank Professor Badiru for his time, dedication, efforts, and selfless work to promote, specifically, Saint Finbarr's College's local, national and international football players, the school's history and successes as "conquerors" of the Principal Cup in Lagos, Nigeria. We have a very rich and respected program, when it comes to footballing talent. Father Slattery was intentional about this. Kudos for promoting this enviable legacy. This is highly recommended for all readers, globally. Good luck and all the best.

Paul Okoku
January 2, 2023

ACKNOWLEDGEMENTS

I gratefully acknowledge the many years of Finbarr's fellowship and fidelity with my fellow alumni of Saint Finbarr's College. In particular, I would like to thank Paul Okoku, one of the greatest soccer players of Finbarr's, whose proactive provision of personal Finbarr's testimonials, professional data, and photos facilitated the constant incentive for me to get this book completed and published. His submissions were instrumental in creating the literary framework for this book.

LIST OF FINBARR'S SOCCER PLAYERS OVER THE DECADES

Powerful names have played soccer for Saint Finbarr's College over the decades. For the same of promoting Finbarr's Fellowship, the list below (subject to corrections and updates) recognizes and celebrates Finbarr's soccer players from the 1960s, 1970s, 1980s, 1990s, 2000s, 2010s, and 2020s.

1.	Abiodun Jide Idowu (Jen Cut)	17.	Bello Kunta
2.	Abudu Momoh	18.	Benedict Oyobio
3.	Ademola Segun Fetuga	19.	Benson Ajighevi
4.	Aghenu Okpanachi	20.	Bernard Senaya (Baba Alli)
5.	Akinyosoye	21.	Cajetan Obinatu
6.	Alani Farawe	22.	Charles Ajighevi
7.	Alex Agbedetse	23.	Charles Chizea
8.	Alex Kofi	24.	Chris Anigala
9.	Amaechi Nwogu	25.	Chris Oyobio
10.	Anthony Daniel	26.	Chris Uwajie
11.	Anthony Mbong	27.	Cosmos Irhurhe
12.	Anthony Orji	28.	Cyril Braimoh
13.	Aronu Ogugo (Gorimapa)	29.	Cyril Iweze
14.	Ayanwale Ganiyu	30.	Daisi Adama
15.	B Atalaye	31.	Daisi Adama
16.	Bazooka	32.	Daniel Smart

CHAPTER I

INTRODUCTION

There is no school comparable to Saint Finbarr's College. All the Boys of Finbarr's will proclaim or boast. It turns out that this is not just an empty boast, but an accurate proclamation. So much so that an "old Boy" of Finbarr's, Nathaniel Ogedegbe, rightfully affirm that Finbarr's is "The best high school above all high schools on the planet." Those who have experienced Finbarr's firsthand or through its diverse impacts can joyfully confirm this statement. In this book, I will explain why this statement is true and why all Boys of Finbarr's abide by this exalted expectation. Casual observers may snicker about this claim; however, a direct observation will make believers out of naysayers. An analogy from the sales and marketing industry claims "a view will convince you." It is a documented fact that graduates of the school have made remarkable impacts in various sectors of society, ranging from sports, medicine, business, academia, industry, government, the military, and politics. I am appreciative that my Finbarr's colleagues recognized me with the Distinguished Conqueror (DC) award in 1998. This is a recognition that I greatly value. My DC plaque, shown below, has occupied a special display consistently in my home since it was received.

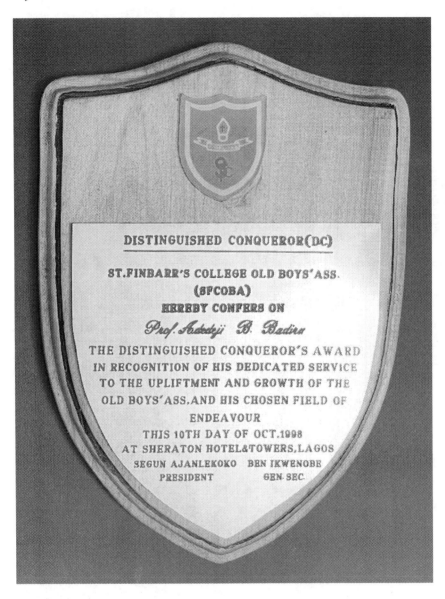

THE PURPOSE OF THIS BOOK

Why is this book needed? While there is much to write about the diverse accomplishments of ex-Finbarrians (aka Old Boys, Conquerors), the purpose of this present book is to salute, recognize, and celebrate the special group of Finbarr's Students, the soccer players (the footballers, if we wish to subscribe to the British moniker). Much has been written about the accomplishments of other groups of ex-Finbarrians, but nothing has been written collectively about our footballers. This book represents the first crack towards achieving the goal of having dedicated book to Finbarr's footballers. We know many of the former Finbarr's players, but we cannot take it for granted that we know all of their sports exploits. This book helps to bring to light the diverse accomplishments of the individual players while at Finbarr's and after Finbarr's. For example, it was a big delight for me, as the author of this book, to discover the tremendous track record of Paul Okoku. Seeing the modesty that permeates the persona of the former players that we socialize with, we may never realize the depth and breadth of their accomplishments. Writing this book has been very enlightening for me and I hope it will be equally enlightening for readers.

Although many of the soccer greats of Finbarr's are known through oral tradition of telling stories about the school's soccer achievements and the exemplary performances of the individual players, it is a fact that the oral history will fade with the passage of time, particularly as the oral chroniclers pass on to the other world. It is, thus, important to have an archival written documentation that future generations can read for the purpose of gloating about the soccer greatness of Saint Finbarr's College.

FOUNDATIONAL LEGACY OF SAINT FINBARR'S COLLEGE

The premise and theme advanced by this book form the unique trifecta of expectations at Saint Finbarr's College:

- Academics
- Discipline
- Sports (Specifically, Soccer)

> **"At Finbarr's, we play what we learn,**
> **we learn what we play."**
>
> – Deji Badiru

ACADEMICS

This is the triple helix structure established by the school's founder, Reverend Father Denis J. Slattery in 1956. This proud structure of expectation still exists today. It has been sustained and preserved by the school administrators who succeeded Father Slattery and the students who are proud to continue to espouse Finbarr's ADS (Academics, Discipline, and Sports). We can even venture to opine that Finbarr's ADS adds much to each student's life. The nexus of excellence that is deeply rooted at Finbarr's is depicted in the graphic below.

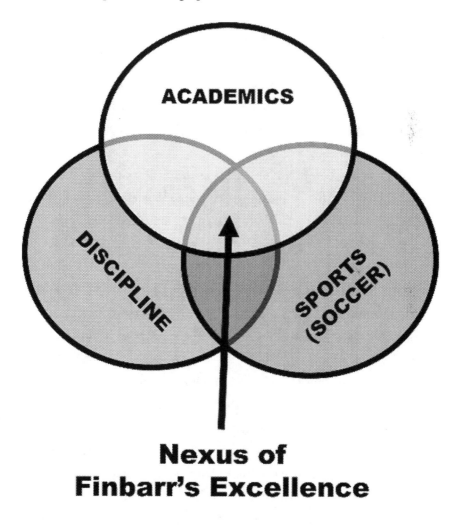

Nexus of Finbarr's Excellence

I was fortunate to have been taught by Father Slattery himself in 1968-1970. He taught Religious Studies. His style of teaching was replete with storytelling both from the Bible and from real-life social settings. He came into class nonchalantly without any notes, chalk, or folders. He sat at the edge of the instructor's desk and embarked upon stories in ways that captured the student's attention with the compelling message that facilitated acquisition and retention of knowledge. I clearly recall my classroom interactions with him with respect to two specific topics that I have never forgotten: The Immaculate Conception and The Prodigal Son. The way he told the stories (i.e., lectures) made students want to hear more. If he caught a student not paying rapt attention to his lectures, he unleashed his wrath onto the whole class. He'd shout, jump, and gesticulate while praying for a better future for all his Finbarr's students. He pumped up his diminutive frame as if puffing up to engage a student in a physical fight. He was a remarkable attention-grabber, and of course he grabbed mine. I never forgot any of his lectures. I credited his style to my success in the WAEC (West African Examination Council) external exam in 1972, even though I was not particularly interested in religious studies in those days. In preparation for the external examination, I recalled all of Father Slattery's classroom stories without resorting to any additional readings. One story was about the biblical story of the Prodigal Son. The way Father Slattery recounted the story, it would be hard for anyone to forget it: *In the gospel of Luke, Jesus tells the well-known parable of the prodigal son. A son asks his father for his inheritance, then squanders it recklessly as he lives a life of indulgence. With nothing left of his fortune, he is forced to work as a hired hand for a pig farmer.*With this kind of superior classroom performance, Father Slattery contributed directly to the academic legacy of Saint Finbarr's College. Thus, Academics, Discipline, and Sports took an indelible root at the school, and they can still be observed in the present day. Father Slattery told Biblical stories (i.e., class lectures) as if he was there in person and he put the intended lessons in the context of what he expected his students to achieve in life as upright citizens. He used his "bully pulpit" effectively in ways that one can hardly forget the lessons he imparted. I gained several lifelong academic benefits from Saint Finbarr's College.

A photo of my Finbarr's Class IIIA in 1970 is shown below. Although some of those in the photo are dearly departed, many of us have remained in close contact and reside in different parts of the world.

Front row (kneeling) left to right:

Richard Egbaiyelo, Sodunke Babajide, Oluwole Cole, Michael Elumeze, Benedict Ikwenobe, Abimbola Aibinu, Ernest Ndiwe (late), Femi Dos Reis

Second row- left to right:

Mr. A. A. Kpotie (Biology Teacher), Joseph Obasa, Charles Hazoume, Ekong Udoffia (late), Wale Adewoyin, Francis Egbuniwe (late), Olayinka Sanni (late), Bodunde Badiru, Babatunde Ogunde, Ayodele Omokoya, Jonathan Egboh (late), Femi Olanrewaju (late), Joseph Molokwu, Visiting teacher from NCE (National College of Education)

Back row- left to right:

Emmanuel Nwaise, Joseph Olisemeka, Pius Danso, Emmanuel Ohikere, Anthony Edem, Adetola Alimi, Adegboyega Solarin, Felix Membu (late), Layiwola Ladenegan, Onofiok Ufot, Philip Bieni, Babatunde Akinwunmi, Akinsola Akinsete (snr).

As a confirmation of the academic depth of my Finbarr's experience, a consolidated image of my artistically-customized and inscribed notebook covers is provided below for my three science subjects of the day: Physics, Chemistry, and Biology. These notebooks were popular with my instructors and classmates. It was customary for classmates to borrow my class notes for the purpose of building their own study notes. These notes were so useful that I still occasionally refer to the contents for current scientific elucidation. I often take the notebooks to Finbarr's reunion events, as show-and-tell displays, with much delight and appreciation by fellow Finbarrians.

FINBARR'S STRUCTURED EDUCATIONAL PROCESS

The educational process established by Father Slattery is based on the structure of Input, Process, and Output, as depicted graphically below. There is a solid Catholic Education Culture, which serves as the foundation for academics. Under the mandate of discipline, students are molded towards several personal attributes, chief among which are social responsibility and character building. The commitment to sports, specifically, soccer, guide students along the path of teamwork and commitment to society needs and benefits. All students follow this rigid structure and are, forever, blessed by the Finbarr's experience. All students of Saint Finbarr's College are linked by the commitment to the school's motto of ***Fidelitas***.

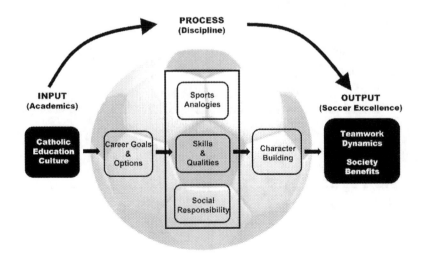

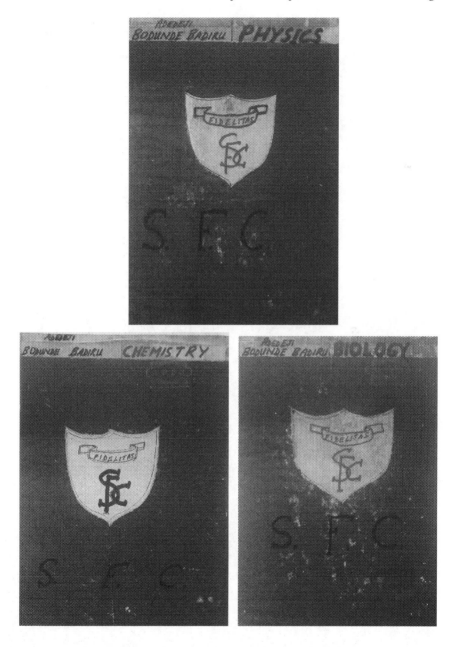

Father Slattery took personal interest in the academic performance, progress, and success of each and every student. A testament to this are the two testimonial documents that he provided to me upon my graduation.

NO 08504/016

DATE 6th Dec. 1972

LEAVING CERTIFICATE & TESTIMONIAL

NAME BODUNDE BADIRU

DATE OF BIRTH 2nd September, 1952

TIME SPENT IN THIS COLLEGE January, 1968 – December, 1972

SUBJECTS STUDIED :- Religion, English Language, Art, French, Biology, Chemistry, Physics, Maths and Add. Maths.

STANDARD PASSED Secondary Class Five

CONDUCT Satisfactory

OTHER REMARKS : Very well behaved; should succeed. Member of the French Club, Art Societyand Quiz Club.

SAINT FINBARR'S COLLEGE PRINCIPAL
AKOKA, YABA ST. FINBARR'S COLLEGE
YABA

Date

Faith Printing Press, EB, Phone 44719

ST. FINBARR'S COLLEGE
AKOKA VILLAGE, YABA.

Our Ref No. SFC/P/-/73/74
Your Ref No.....................
Our Phone No 47855

P. O. Box 478,
YABA,
LAGOS, NIGERIA.

8th February, 1974

TO WHOM IT MAY CONCERN

Badiru Badunde was a student of St. Finbarr's College from January 1968 to December, 1972; during which he took a five years course in secondary subjects - both Grammar and Science.

He was very well behaved and above average academically. He had an excellent result in his first public examinations - the West African School Certificate.

His character was most satisfactory.

Rev. Father D. J. Slattery.
ST. FINBARR'S COLLEGE
Akoka - Yaba
Date..............................

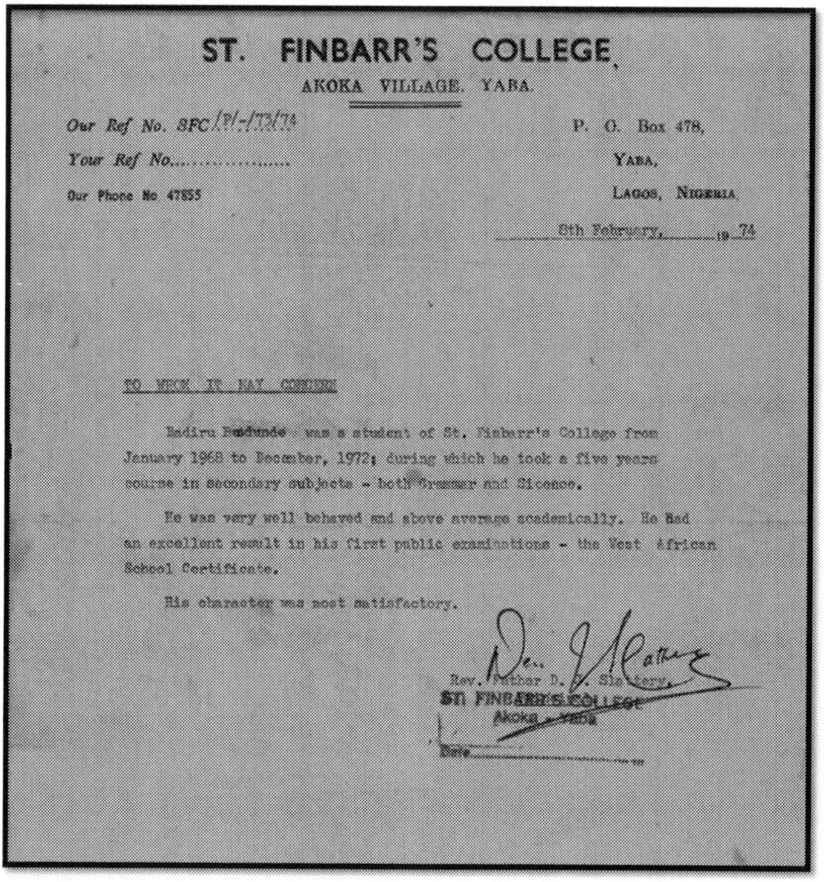

Also shown here is a photo of our Physics Lab in 1971. I appear second from the left in the photo. My now-famous classmate, Dr. Ayodele Omokoya, a medical doctor in Lagos, is the first from the right in the photo. Richard Egbaiyelo, Felix Membu, late Olayinka Sanni and late Francis Egbuniwe are the other students in the photo. It was not all work and no play at Finbarr's.

Finbarr's Physics Lab (1971)

In spite of Father Slattery's watchful eyes and disciplined demeanor, the boys always found a way to break loose and have fun within and outside the school compound. A photo reproduced here shows some of my classmates and me in unrestrained photo sessions.

Another testament to Father's Slatter's total commitment to Academics alongside Discipline and Sports is that when my WASC (West African School Certificate) result came out with a Grade I Distinction category, he personally, in his unorthodox way, sent an underclass Finbarr's student to my neighborhood in Ebute-Metta to announce the result to everyone. Thus, in a society where education was valued and celebrated, I became an instant darling among the neighborhood kids. Father Slattery was so proud of the result that he gloated about it for several months, along with the other similarly superior results from Finbarr's. Father Slatter's commitment to Academics was unrivalled and he let everyone around Lagos know it. He claimed that with a Finbarr's education, kids cannot go wrong and he put his entire life behind that commitment. Academic excellence ruled (and still rules) at Saint Finbarr's College.

West African Examinations Council

School Certificate

NOVEMBER 1972

This is to Certify that: BADIRU BODUNDE

having been in attendance at the following recognised school

ST. FINBARR'S COLLEGE, AKOKA YABA

sat the Joint Examination for the School Certificate and General Certificate of Education and qualified for the award of a School Certificate.

The Candidate obtained the following results

SUBJECT	GRADE	SCHOOL CERTIFICATE RESULT	G.C.E. ORDINARY LEVEL EQUIVALENT
ENGLISH LANGUAGE	1	EXCELLENT	PASS
FRENCH	1	EXCELLENT	PASS
MATHEMATICS	2	VERY GOOD	PASS
ADDITIONAL MATHEMATICS	6	CREDIT	PASS
PHYSICS	3	GOOD	PASS
CHEMISTRY	6	CREDIT	PASS
BIOLOGY	3	GOOD	PASS
ART	2	VERY GOOD	PASS
RELIGIOUS KNOWLEDGE	3	GOOD	PASS
SUBJECTS RECORDED		NINE	NINE

DIVISION 1 DISTINCTION   CD 60

CANDIDATE No. 08504016

CERTIFICATE No. SC057988

Registrar to the Council

Any alteration or erasure renders this certificate valueless.

As a further demonstration of the Academics legacy of Saint Finbarr's College, SFCOBA (Saint Finbarr's Old Boys Association), under the leadership and sponsorship of Mr. Segun Ajanlekoko, published a quarterly newsletter, named The Finbarrians consistently in the 1990s. A page sample from the newsletter is provided here.

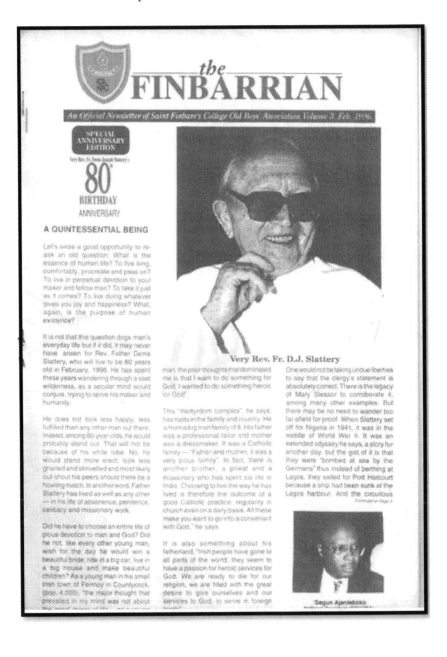

I have been fortunate that my Finbarr's Classmates have recognized and celebrated me on the academic and professional sides for many years, as shown in the DC (Distinguished Conqueror) award and The Father Slattery Award photos below. I am very grateful for all the non-sports-related accolades I have received from my Fellow Finbarrians.

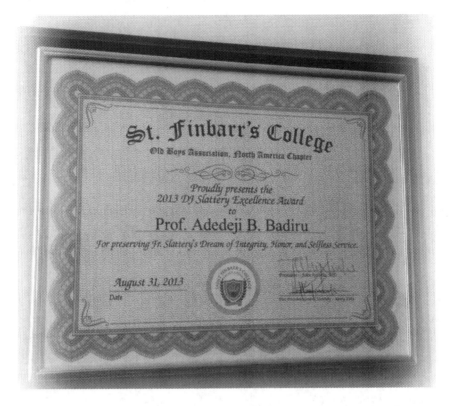

DISCIPLINE

The pursuit of *discipline* was like a religion at Saint Finbarr's College. Certainly the atmosphere of a Catholic School was in the air, but Father Slattery did not run the school as a religious school. It was an all-inclusive school, where academically-qualified pupils of any religion, creed, or social-economic background could attend as long as they demonstrated the discipline to apply themselves to the task at hand. Without reservation, Father Slattery admitted and embraced children from all walks of life, which was how I was admitted to the school. He admitted several Muslim students and he did not attempt to convert them to Christianity or Catholicism. Instead, he encouraged all students to doggedly pursue their respective avowed religions. In fact, he gave Muslim students a special pass to leave the school compound on Friday afternoons to engage in the traditional Friday Muslim prayers. For this reason, some students jokingly (or mischievously) declared themselves to be of the Muslim faith. Father Slattery expected each student to demonstrate the discipline to do the right thing by declaring accurately and faithfully. With discipline and self-control, any student could apply his natural talent and intelligence to achieve whatever he set out to pursue. Therefore, many soccer players at Finbarr's excelled. They applied their school-imbibed discipline to maximize their sports performance. Without discipline, even the most skilled person cannot be successful. Father Slattery strived to keep the "Boys" in line through mandatory discipline. In fact, the lessons learnt from Finbarr's ADS influenced the writing of my book entitled *Badiru's Equation of Student Success: Intelligence, Common Sense, and Self-Discipline.* In this book, the following relational equation was introduced:

$$\textbf{\textit{Success}} = \textbf{\textit{f(x, y, z)}}$$

Success is a function of three elements:

x: intelligence
y: common sense
z: self-discipline

Natural intelligence is no good to anyone if there is no self-discipline to apply to the intelligence. The efficacy of this simple equation has been confirmed again and again through direct practical observations. I have benefited from the dictate contained in the equation. I know it works. Parents, over the years, have also confirmed their belief in the equation.

It goes without saying that the great soccer players that came out of Finbarr's benefited from the school's intertwined legacy of academics, discipline, and soccer. Many of Finbarr's soccer players went on to play professionally, play for the Nigerian national team, or coached competitively at the national level. Soccer is an anchor at Saint Finbarr's College. My previous books published about Finbarr's, Soccer, and related motivational topics were inspired by the Finbarr's legacy of academics, discipline, and sports that I benefited from. Those books are listed below.

1. **More Physics of Soccer: Playing the Game Smart and Safe**, iUniverse, Bloomington, Indiana, 2022.
2. *My Everlasting Education at Saint Finbarr's College: Academics, Discipline, and Sports*, iUniverse, Bloomington, Indiana, USA, 2020
3. *The Story of Saint Finbarr's College: Father Slattery's Contributions to Education and Sports in Nigeria,* iUniverse, Bloomington, Indiana, USA, 2018
4. *Physics of Soccer II: Science and Strategies for a Better Game*, iUniverse, Bloomington, Indiana, USA, 2018
5. *Youth Soccer Training Slides: A Math and Science Approach*, iUniverse, Bloomington, Indiana, USA, 2014
6. *Badiru's Equation of Student Success: Intelligence, Common Sense, and Self-Discipline*, iUniverse, Bloomington, Indiana, USA, 2013
7. *Blessings of a Father: Education contributions of Father Slattery at Saint Finbarr's College,* iUniverse, Bloomington, Indiana, USA, 2013
8. *Physics of Soccer: Using Math and Science to Improve Your Game*, iUniverse, Bloomington, Indiana, USA, 2010
9. *Blessings of a Father: A Tribute to the Life and Work of Reverend Father Denis J. Slattery*, Heriz Designs and Prints, Lagos, Nigeria, 2005

This present book complements the previous books above. This is the first book that focuses on explicit tributes for Finbarr's soccer players. The discipline that governed the lives of the soccer players while they played for Finbarr's has continued to serve every individual well in their personal professional and career paths after Finbarr's. We can say that Life After Finbarr's has been good for every Finbarr's soccer player. May discipline continue to reign in all our lives, just as Father Slattery intended it to be.

SOCCER

Soccer is the representative sport at Saint Finbarr's College. When sports are mentioned at Finbarr's, soccer is the de facto reference, although the school embraced diverse participation in other sports. Soccer is the sport of Finbarr's. Father Slattery is shown in the photo below, congratulating players at a national game in the early 1970s. Many times, Finbarr's soccer teams, celebrated victories, thus affirming Finbarr's soccer supremacy.

The FIFA 2022 Soccer World Cup tournament reaffirmed the worldwide phenomenon and momentum of sports in society. The 2022 FIFA World Cup tournament has been described as the tournament for the ages. Although there have been many great tournaments before. Teams from the Arab block and the African continent did well in the tournament, particularly in the early stages. The stunning defeat of Argentina by Saudi Arabia reverberated throughout the sports world. The eventual success of Argentina in winning the World Cup seemed to right the ship in the end. The match-for-match contest between Lionel Messi of Argentina and Kylian Mbappé of France brought a heightened attention to the tournament. These are two of the best soccer players in the world. The triumph of Messi at the age of 35 over the relative youngster, Mbappe at the age of 23 brought a renewed hope for aging athletes. The tournament was projected as Messi's last gasp for a World Cup championship and he succeeded even though pundits had written him off earlier. It was a great story of a reversed fortune.

Brazilian soccer legend, Pelé (born Edson Arantes do Nascimento) has an enduring legacy that has fueled soccer's interest and growth around the world for decades. He made his debut as a 17-year-old player and dazzled the world with his skills and tenacity. He led Brazil to victory in the 1958, 1962, and 1970 World Cups. In the Nigerian soccer context, the names of Pelé and Muhammad Ali (born Cassius Clay) continue to provide sports inspiration to thousands of youths. It is interesting that the peaks of their sports careers overlapped in the 1960s and 1970s. Unlike many other popular sports, soccer is a sport of the common man. Thousands of common kids used Pele and Ali as benchmarks of how to reach stardom, particularly from the underserved communities of society. Many young soccer players at Finbarr's aspired to be like Pele. Their striving paid off in many respects as many former Finbarr's soccer players went on to make their own marks around the world.

During the 2022 World Cup, an entertaining social media post emerged to confirm that every one of the 32 national teams that started the competition had at least one player of African origin or descent on the team. Therein lies the role that Africa played in the 2022 World Cup. As an example, the popular French player, Kylian Mbappe, is of African descent. His father is of Cameroonian origin, while his mother, a former handball player, is of Algerian origin. Although Nigeria did not qualify for the 2022 World Cup, the past and the expected future participation of Nigeria took center stage in many discussions by soccer sports connoisseurs. Nigeria shall return.

2022 WORLD CUP QUALIFIERS

- **UEFA** (Union of European Football Associations) - 13 Countries: Belgium, Croatia, Denmark, England, France, Germany, Netherlands, Poland, Portugal, Serbia, Spain, Switzerland, Wales

- **AFC** (Asian Football Confederation) – 6 Countries: Australia, Iran, Japan, Qatar (hosts), Saudi Arabia, South Korea
- **CAF** (Confederation of African Football) – 5 Countries: Cameroon, Ghana, Morocco, Senegal, Tunisia
- **CONMEBOL** (Confederacion Sudamericana de Futbol; South American Football Confederation) – 4 Countries: Argentina, Brazil, Ecuador, Uruguay
- **CONCAF** (Confederation of North, Central America and Caribbean Association Football) – 4 Countries: Canada, Costa Rica, Mexico, USA

Whither Art Thou, Nigeria's football? May the past force of Finbarr's soccer return to propel Nigeria to future international competition.

WORLD SOCCER HISTORY

The intersection of soccer with many human pursuits can be used to explain the advancement of society in terms of teamwork, leadership, fitness, collegiality, field geometry, principles of physics, human factors, science, biometrics, and so on. The historical accounts of soccer presented here, comically as some of them are, are culled from various web sources, both official and unofficial. Although many of the accounts are unsubstantiated, they, nonetheless, offer an entertaining glimpse of the origin and evolution of soccer. The game of soccer, known as Football in most parts of the world, has a long and illustrious history. The "original" origin of the game has always been debatable. It is obvious that the game originated at a time of limited written records. Hence, the fuzziness of when the first soccer game took place. Since all humans evolve with the basic instinct of kicking things around, it is the view of this book that soccer-like games evolved gradually and simultaneously in different parts of the world. Soccer, as we know it today, was reportedly first played as a game in England in the mid-19th Century. It appears, though, that soccer's origin goes further back.

Different countries, groups of people, and individuals have offered opinions, albeit from biased viewpoints, on who invented games involving the use of feet and a ball. The International Federation of Association Football, **Fédération Internationale de Football Association** (FIFA) has an article about the history of soccer that credits the Chinese with inventing the game. The only documented reference to the origin of soccer is from the observations of Greek historian Herodotus of Halicarnassus (5ᵗʰ Century, BCE, Before Common Era, replacement for A.D.) who described a game played by soldiers where the defeated team captain's head would be severed, dipped in melted rubber, and used for the play of the rematch. Some other unsubstantiated "fun" claims that have been reported in online postings include the following (culled from various sources (authors unknown):

- "It started in Brazil when a few children were playing together when they saw a bucket of soft rubber which came from a rubber plantation nearby. Then, one of them got an idea and turned it into a ball-shape. So, the children played with each other but not in the modern way. They just pass each other without touching with their hands. Some tourist nearby happened to pass by and saw what had happened and decided to change the game with two goal post and 20 aside."
- "Soccer was first played as a game by Roman soldiers, who used the heads of their enemies in a game with simple goalposts. So it's understandable why there is a rule against touching the ball with your hands. Just kick it again."
- "It began in Italy with small rocks, we now call Bacchic ball, played by the Roman soldiers when bored at their post, progressed to larger rocks, then due to the difficulty in the weight, material was sewn together to form a large ball. Each century there were modifications made, until today."
- "Soccer came to Europe from the Mexicans; after a battle they would chop off their opponents' heads and use them as football. This form

of entertainment was then taken across to Europe by the Spaniards, Portuguese, Dutch, and so on. only"

- "The historical origin of soccer was in China in about 2600 BC. They used a ball made of leather. The goals were about 30 feet high and 20 feet apart and was played in celebration of the emperor's birthday. The name was called Tsi chu. It was played during the Hun Dynasty."

- "Soccer was invented by the Mayan and Aztec Indians in Central America. At the Mayan Ruins, in the city of Copan, Honduras, they had one of the first soccer fields ever. This civilization dates back to more than 10,000 years ago. In this civilization, Soccer teams would compete against each other and the captain of the winning team was sacrificed after the game. The act of being sacrificed was considered an honor to these people."

- From the history of soccer page at About.com: "There is documentary evidence that a a game or skill building exercise, involving kicking a ball into a small net, was used by the Chinese military during the Han Dynasty - around the 2nd and 3rd centuries BC. Earlier evidence - of a field marked out to play a ball-kicking game has been found at Kyoto, in Japan. Both the Greeks and ancient Romans played a soccer-type game which resembled modern soccer - although in this early version, teams could consist of up to 27 players!"

- "It is believed that the first recorded soccer game took place on a Shrove Tuesday in Derby, England, as part of a festival to celebrate the victory of English soldiers over Roman troops (AD 217). By 1175 the annual Shrove Tuesday soccer game was a regular event."

- "It is correct that a lot of games were played in the history of mankind where something was kicked around. As well as tennis, volleyball or hacky sack are not simply defined by the fact that a ball is played over a net, soccer is not defined by trying to kick something into whatever goal. The game we know as soccer today was founded in the English public schools in the early 19th century by simple school boys that played the game although it was mostly forbidden. They discussed and changed the rules of the game. Later the games were allowed and seen as good training for manhood and fairness. To give an extra challenge to fair play and self-control, the boys of Eton forbade the use of the hands. As not being allowed to use the hands is the main characteristic of soccer in contrast to rugby, it appears that was the moment when soccer was born. Soccer and Rugby parted and went different ways; and the former became the sport we know as soccer today. Soccer later spread to the continent, where the first national game was Austria against Hungary."

• "Soccer was believed by scientists to have been started in the Chinese Han Dynasty in 1000 B.C. They think that it was played by the military to make sure that the soldiers were ready for battle. It was later played in the Roman and Greek civilizations, but with many more players and not that many rules. It is known for a fact that "soccer" was played in 600 A.D. in Kyoto, Japan. Later, football was played in the United Kingdom by people of all sorts. The king of England thought that soccer should be banned because of how dangerous it was, but no one could stop soccer because it had become too popular of a sport. Today soccer is all over the world and considered to be the most popular sport of all."

THE FORCE OF FINBARR'S OLD BOYS

All the good and exciting stories of the 2022 World Cup gave me the final incentive and momentum for completing this manuscript, which I actually started in August 2019 during the North America alumni reunion of Saint Finbarr's College in Dayton, Ohio. As the local host of the reunion, I announced my intention to write such a book and I invited our "old Boys" to provide inputs and suggestions. The former soccer players of Finbarr's were particularly encouraged to provide details of their Finbarr's soccer exploits that could be recognized and celebrated in the book. **Paul Okoku**, an extraordinary player at Finbarr's, was the first to answer the call for inputs. He remained committed and supportive throughout the manuscript-development project. In fact, his commitment to seeing the book completed added to the motivation for me to deliver on my 2019 promise.

The final drive to complete this Finbarr's soccer-tribute book was the December 2022 shocking death of **Bernard Senaya** (July 12, 1950 – December 5, 2022), a Finbarr's soccer maestro in his days at the school. He attended the reunion in Dayton, Ohio and had pledged his support for the book project. In fact, in our follow-up conversation about the project, he agreed to be interviewed for contents of his Finbarr's story to be included in the book. We both procrastinated on scheduling the one-on-one interview. His unexpected death before we could do the interview confirmed the adage that "Do today what you can do today. Do not procrastinate until tomorrow." Thus, I embarked on finishing the manuscript the very day that I heard of Bernard's eternal departure. May his soul rest in perfect peace.

ADIEU TO BERNARD SENAYA

I was happy and proud that the Saint Finbarr's College Old Boys Association (SFCOBA) held a celebration of life in honor of Bernard Senaya at the Finbarr's school campus on December 22nd 2022. The Finbarr's campus funeral event was extraordinarily organized, orchestrated, and executed. It was attended by the present and past presidents of SFCOBA, namely **Patrick Doyle**, **Yinka Bashorun**, and **Segun Ajanlekoko**. They, as well as others, presented rousing accounts and tributes in honor of

Bernard. The glowing tribute written by John Senaya, Bernard's younger brother is provided in the appendix of this book. The tribute not only profiled Bernard's life, but also highlighted how Saint Finbarr's College prepared him for his life of exemplary service.

In Bernard's honor, the soccer ball, like a specter of office, featured prominently throughout the program. Befittingly, it was even placed on the casket in Bernard's final journey.

During his own talk, Segun Ajanlekoko referred to Saint Finbarr's College as the "***Citadel of Learning***," which aptly confirms the premise of this book.

WHY SOCCER MATTERS AT FINBARR'S

As a popular proverb goes, "All work and no play make Jack a dull boy." Father Slattery had the foresight to create an educational template that has permeated the operation of the school for over the past six decades. The crux of that visionary foresight was sports, specifically football (soccer). Now that Jack has been rescued from being dull with the diversion of sports engagement, Father Slattery, true to his Catholic clergy background, now added "discipline" (i.e., uprightness and self-control) to the requirements of the school. So was born the triple helix of the Finbarr's legacy. Many schools have reputations in a combination or permutation of the three elements, as well as other desirables. Finbarr's is unique in the sense that Father Slattery's concept thrived on the three fundamental elements of Academics, Discipline, and Sports. He belief was that all other educational desirables could be accomplished if these three elements were secured. He has been proven right for decades by graduates of Saint Finbarr's College and their contributions throughout the world in diverse fields of pursuits. Some notable examples include the late Bernard Senaya, who not only contributed to Finbarr's soccer exploits, but also went on to play significant corporate leadership roles in the international airline industry. He worked for the Lufthansa German Airlines, Segun Ajanlekoko, who, as a world-renowned entrepreneur and corporate leader, was granted a unique audience by Queen Elizabeth of England in 2015. He was the only ex-Finbarrian to have accomplished that feat (see photo inset). Professor Adedeji Badiru rose through the educational academic ranks to be appointed as the Dean of Engineering at the U.S. Air Force Institute of Technology He was the first black person to reach that exalted position and served ten remarkable years in that leadership role. Patrick Doyle achieved celebrity status as an orator and actor in the entertainment industry. Nathaniel Ogedegbe capitalized on his Finbarr's soccer prowess to create a youth soccer training program in Virginia. Paul Okoku created programs to assist and facilitate youth development, as the Founder and Chief Executive Officer (CEO) of the Greater Tomorrow Children's Fund in the state of Georgia (see photo inset). Dr. John Nwofia gladly exports his medical expertise to care for patients, not only in the U.S., but also in Nigeria.

In his 2014 book, "Why Soccer Matters," the great soccer player, Pele, highlighted why soccer is essential in the socio-economic development of a nation. The politics, economics, and legalities of soccer reverberate throughout all the corners of the world. The intrigue and drama presented by the 2022 FIFA World Cup tournament confirmed why soccer matters. It matters to the world, and it matters at Saint Finbarr's College. Soccer brings people together and it matters in many aspects of world affairs.

Whenever Nigeria participates in the FIFA World Cup competition, the nation is sure to rise up in unison, not only to support and cheer the players, but also to felicitate with one another, regardless of any prevailing socio-economic-political divisions. This was aptly demonstrated in the 1994 World Cup, as demonstrated by the Nigeria Super Eagles ribbon displayed earlier in this chapter.

REFERENCES FOR CHAPTER I

1. Pele with Brian Winter (2014), **Pele: Why Soccer Matter**, Penguin Group, New York, NY.
2. Badiru, Deji (2022), **More Physics of Soccer: Playing the Game Smart and Safe**, iUniverse, Bloomington, Indiana, 2022.
3. Badiru, Deji (2020), *My Everlasting Education at Saint Finbarr's College: Academics, Discipline, and Sports*, iUniverse, Bloomington, Indiana, USA, 2020
4. Badiru, Deji (2018), *The Story of Saint Finbarr's College: Father Slattery's Contributions to Education and Sports in Nigeria,* iUniverse, Bloomington, Indiana, USA, 2018
5. Badiru, Deji (2018), *Physics of Soccer II: Science and Strategies for a Better Game*, iUniverse, Bloomington, Indiana, USA, 2018
6. Badiru, Deji (2014), *Youth Soccer Training Slides: A Math and Science Approach*, iUniverse, Bloomington, Indiana, USA, 2014
7. Badiru, Deji (2013), *Badiru's Equation of Student Success: Intelligence, Common Sense, and Self-Discipline*, iUniverse, Bloomington, Indiana, USA, 2013

8. Badiru, Deji (2013), ***Blessings of a Father: Education contributions of Father Slattery at Saint Finbarr's College,*** iUniverse, Bloomington, Indiana, USA, 2013

9. Badiru, Deji (2010), ***Physics of Soccer: Using Math and Science to Improve Your Game***, iUniverse, Bloomington, Indiana, USA, 2010

10. Badiru, Deji (2005), ***Blessings of a Father: A Tribute to the Life and Work of Reverend Father Denis J. Slattery***, Heriz Designs and Prints, Lagos, Nigeria, 2005

CHAPTER 2

ORIGIN OF SAINT FINBARR'S COLLEGE

The legendary stories of the accomplishments of Saint Finbarr's former soccer players must be told, not just through oral testimonies, but through dedicated archival records. This book does just that. It is hoped that other literary documentations will be pursued and circulated by other writers. It is important that an insider, a former student of Finbarr's be the first one to write a book on the soccer prowess and professional accomplishments of Finbarr's former soccer players. If we don't tout our own Finbarr's horn, no one else will do it for us (from another school).

Of course, Reverend Father Denis J. Slattery was responsible for all that the current and former students of Saint Finbarr's have accomplished. It is appropriate to start the book with an introductory coverage of the life and great deeds of Father Slattery in Nigeria.

The life and time of Father Slattery in Nigeria facilitated and enabled the rapid development of soccer excellence, not only in Lagos, Nigeria, but throughout the nation. By extension, soccer around the world also benefited from what came out of Finbarr's. Beyond the playing field, Finbarr's has made tremendous contributions in various professional fields around the world. This book is about the story of Finbarr's products in soccer and other fields.

Reverend Father Denis Joseph Slattery (February
29, 1916 – July 7, 2003, Age 87)

Denis Slattery was born in Fermoy, Co Cork, in the diocese of Cloyne, on February 29th, 1916. He died in St. Theresa's Unit, Blackrock Road, Cork, on July 7th, 2003.

Denis was one of six boys and two girls born to Catherine and Timothy Francis Slattery. He was born on the odd day of a leap year in 1916 – a momentous year for Ireland - both circumstances in which he took great relish. His family home was located at 65 MacCurtain Street, Fermoy.

Denis received his secondary education from the Christian Brothers in Fermoy (1928-1932) and at St Joseph's College, Wilton, matriculating in 1934. He was promoted to the Society's novitiate and house of philosophy at Kilcolgan, Co Galway. Two years later he entered the Society's major seminary at Dromantine, Newry, Co Down. Denis was received as a member of the Society on June 29th, 1936. He was ordained to priesthood in St. Colman's Cathedral by Bishop Edward Mulhern of Dromore diocese, on December 17th, 1939. He was one of a group of seven ordained on that day.

After ordination Denis was appointed to the Vicariate of Bight of Benin. Due to the difficulties in obtaining a sea passage during wartime he did not reach Nigeria until May 1941. The convoy in which he travelled was bombed by German planes off L'Havre and several ships were sunk. Upon arrival Denis was assigned to Ilawe-Ekiti mission where he studied Yoruba. Six months later he was appointed to the staff of St. Gregory's College in Lagos. This was Nigeria's first Catholic secondary school, founded in 1928. Upon completion of two academic years – during which, in addition to his teaching work, he distinguished himself as Games Master – Denis was appointed Manager of St. Paul's Press and Bookshop at Ebute-Metta. He spent the last two years of his first missionary tour as Editor of the Nigerian Catholic Herald, based in Yaba. Denis' success in this latter capacity led his Superiors to send him to the Catholic University of America, Washington D.C. in January 1947. He majored in Sociology, Journalism and Economics and he was awarded a Master of Arts degree by this institution in 1949. The title of his Master's thesis was 'The Transition from slavery to a free Labour Movement in Nigeria, 1850-1948'.

Upon his return to Nigeria in September 1949 Denis renewed his editorship of the Nigerian Catholic Herald. A monthly magazine when he first became editor, Denis turned the Herald into what he described as 'a militant anti-colonial religious and political weekly.' Indeed, this newspaper became important in molding public opinion in the lead up to Nigerian Independence bringing Denis into close and friendly contact with leading Nigerian Nationalists including Dr. Nnamidi Azikiwe. The Herald was particularly influential during the discussions on the Constitutional Conference. Denis also addressed social issues and his published extracts from his MA thesis relating to 'Nigerian Railways' Workers and the killing of the Coal Miners in Enugu', aroused considerable interest. The fearlessness of his reports during the Nigerian Railways Strike of 1948-1949 earned him the plaudits of Nigerians and the hostility of the colonial government. In June 1954 Denis visited America on vacation and took time to raise funds for the Lagos jurisdiction. Six months later he returned to Nigeria. He was to remain in the Lagos jurisdiction until September 1999 when ill health compelled him to reluctantly retire. Overall, he spent about fifty-five years in Nigeria, making him one of the longest-serving missionaries in the Society and one of two members of the Irish Province to give such service.

In 1955 Denis became founding principal of St Finbarr's College which started as a two-classroom building on Apapa Road before moving to its present site at Akoka. Denis was to guide this prestigious school with a sure hand until 1976 when with other Catholic schools were taken over by government. He devoted the remaining years of his missionary career to the pastoral ministry. He ministered in St. Denis Catholic Church, Bariga-Akoka – near his beloved St. Finbarr's - which he built and named. He also built and founded St. Flavius Catholic Church, Oworonshoki, and St. Gabriel's church, Somolu. In addition he established St. Joseph's Vocational School, and Our Lady of Fatima Nursery and Primary School, both in Akoka. In 1985 Denis was appointed Vicar General of Lagos Archdiocese, a post which required him to take charge of the jurisdiction during the Archbishop's absence.

Coming from a family keenly interested in athletics, Denis' enthusiasm was given a very practical and important expression throughout his missionary career. In 1947, he became an accredited referee and a member of the Nigerian Association of Amateur Referees. He also pioneered the training of Nigeria's first indigenous referees. Despite his small stature he radiated authority when in possession of the referee's whistle. As a FIFA graded referee, he took charge of several international matches involving Nigeria and the Gold Coast as well as many FA finals. He took a keen interest in school sports, helping to establish the popular school soccer competition, 'The Principal's Cup' (known popularly as the 'Zard Cup') in 1949. His own school, St. Finbarr's, won this trophy in 1971, 1972 and 1973. Denis was also a member of the Nigerian Amateur Boxing Association. Moreover, putting his journalistic skills to good use, for many years he wrote a Sports Colum in the Lagos Weekend newspaper under the pen-name 'Green Flag'.

Denis received many honors during his life from the people he served so well. In 1989 he was conferred with chieftaincies by Imo State and Ile-Ife State. One of the chieftaincy titles fittingly hailed him as 'Enyi Oha 1 of Oru Ahiara Mbaise' ('Friend of the People'). The second title was that of 'Oosi Olokun-Ijio of Ife'. Denis's long and distinguished service was recognized by the Nigerian government in their National Honors Awards in 2001. He received the Order of the Niger during his retirement. A year later he was honored by the Fermoy Urban Council.

In 1996, to commemorate his 80th birthday, Denis published his memoirs under the title *My Life Story*. This was launched at the Institute of International Affairs in Lagos. His age and status allowed him to speak openly on social, religious and political issues and he was widely reported. From the 1960's he was known as a staunch advocate and encouraging critic of the people of Nigeria in their search for self-expression and self-reliance as a nation.

Denis celebrated the Golden Jubilee of his priesthood in 1989 and his Diamond Jubilee in 1999. The homilist at his funeral Mass said: 'There is no doubt that Denis took great pride in all his achievements. His life was ultimately lived not to bring honor to himself but to give honor and glory to God.' Personally, any story of mine will not be complete without the concomitant story of Saint Finbarr's College. My life is enmeshed with the story of Saint Finbarr's College. There are schools and then there are *schools*, but there is no school like Saint Finbarr's College. This book is the third of mine that discusses Saint Finbarr's College and the monumental contributions of Reverend Father Denis Joseph Slattery. The **Society of African Missions** (SMA) is a Roman Catholic missionary organization in which he was proudly apart of. The society's members come from around the world with a commitment to serve the people of Africa and those of African descent.

Father Slattery came and advanced the nation of Nigeria through his multi-faceted contributions to education, sports, and discipline. His memory will never wane in Nigeria. In this regard, this book documents the continuing efforts of Saint Finbarr's College Old Boys Association (SFCOBA) around the World to enliven the story of the school. This book is written from my personal perspective. Similar stories are often told by other ex-students from their own respective perspectives. All stories have the same similar vein, thus, confirming the consistency of the legacy of Father Slattery. You cannot separate the story of Father Slattery from the story of Saint Finbarr's College and vice versa. Both stories go hand-in-hand.

The story of Saint Finbarr's College is fascinating and inspiring, no matter how many times and different places or formats you have heard the story before. In many instances, the story seems duplicative, but that is good for affirmation and confirmation purposes. When Finbarr's is concerned, repeat is not a violation. The story revolves around the life and deeds of Reverend Denis Joseph Slattery, an Irish-Catholic priest, who came to

Nigeria in 1941 and never left, until his work was finished. In this sense, the term refers to the completion of planting the seeds of success for Saint Finbarr's students. Those seeds continued to germinate and bear fruits even after he left Nigeria in 2003. The tentacles of the positive legacies of Father Slattery and Saint Finbarr's College can be seen all over the world today, as graduates of the school continue to make professional inroads on various platforms around the world.

This book includes the commemoration of the contributions of Father Slattery to education, youth discipline, and sports development in Nigeria. It is designed as an archival reference to many of Finbarr's historical records and accolades. The history of Saint Finbarr's College is a favorite pastime of all the former and present students at the school. Saint Finbarr's is most noted for three characteristics: Academics, Football (soccer), and Discipline. It was in recognition and appreciation of the impacts of the above attributes that I wrote the previous books about Finbarr's. What I am today, professionally, is the product of the educational and disciplinary foundations I acquired at Saint Finbarr's. For this, I remain very grateful. My biographical sketch below sums up the end product of my journey that started at Saint Finbarr's College under the watchful eye and magnanimous deeds of Reverend Father Slattery.

Reverend Father Denis Joseph Slattery came to Nigeria in 1941. Having served in a parish at Ilawe-Ekiti, in the Yoruba Inland Town of Ilawe-Ekiti, Father Slattery was posted to Saint Gregory's College as a teacher and later became the Games Master. He later became the editor of the Catholic Herald in Mushin. It was during this period that the thought of establishing a unique school occurred to him. His school became the first bilateral school in the country, combining full Grammar (called Basic) with Arts and Technical subjects. In the 1955/56 academic year, with six students, fondly referred to as "the first six of the first six", a new unnamed school was born.

The new school had to be accommodated in the newly built St. Paul's Catholic Primary School in Lagos. The next task was to look for a site for the new school. Father Slattery searched eventually reached a wilderness area in Akoka, where he met a man who knew him, but whom he did not know. The friendly disposition of the man made it easy for Father Slattery to acquire a twenty-plot piece of land in the present site of the school. In 1959, the school moved from Apapa Road to its present site in Akoka. In 1963, the school was officially opened by Dr. Nnamdi Azikiwe, the first President of Nigeria, who was a friend of Father Slattery.

In a tactical move, he got a grant from the British colonial government, with which he set up a ten-classroom block, two technical drawing rooms, a technical block, an administrative block, which also housed the teachers staff room, and a dining-room assembly hall with a well-equipped kitchen. Among the first teachers at the school were the late Chief Albert Bankole, Father Slattery, and Mr. F. Ekpeti.

Although a complete and accurate listing of the first set of students is difficult for me to come by at this time, oral accounts indicate that the first set of students, known as Finbarr's First Set (FFS), included very renowned names in Nigeria.

The first National President of SFCOBA, A. Madufor, came from FFS. The second National President was Tom Borha, an editor of Concord Group of Newspapers. The Third National President was M A C Odu, an Estate Surveyor and Valuer. SFCOBA accomplished many things on behalf of Saint Finbarr's College. Land Surveying was conducted to establish the spatial limits of the school permanently. The order of Distinguished Conquerors (DC) was created to recognize distinguished alumni of the school. Tom Borha received the first one. I received the honor in 1998.

The Presidency of SFCOBA shifted from FFS in 1994 when Segun Ajanlekoko was elected. Segun quickly elevated SFCOBA and SFC into more national and international prominence through a variety of high-profile activities and projects. I met Segun around 1995 and we have both remained staunch advocates for SFC. The system of identifying students by their class years was established and advanced by SFCOBA. I belong to the 1972 Set. When Mr. Yinka Bashorun became the national president, he instituted the process of unifying the various branches of SFCOBA domestically and abroad under one National and International SFCOBA. Everyone, to the last man, has been committed to the task of rekindling the glory days of Saint Finbarr's College.

The school made its first attempt at the West African School Certificate Examinations in 1961, having been approved in 1960. In that first attempt, the technical department had 100% passes, with 80% making 3 or 4 credits. Grammar had 50% passes with two of them making distinctions. These boys were also top in sports and Vice-Admiral Patrick Koshoni happened to be one of the two. From then on, the academic results kept improving year after year, with the technical department consistently recording 100% passes. In fact, in those days Grade 1, Grade 2, and Grade 3 categorization of WAEC results, the understanding or common expectation was that all candidates would normally pass and what everybody was interested in was how many came out in Grade One or Grade Two. Grade Three was regarded as a consolation result. This trend remained true until the government takeover of schools in the mid 1970's.

SPORTS EXCELLENCE OF SAINT FINBARR'S COLLEGE

Father Slattery was very eager to put the school at the forefront quickly in football since it would take 5 years for the school to prove its excellence in academics. In its first year, it pitched itself in a football match against its host, St. Paul's Primary School and lost 1-2. In 1957, it St. Gregory's where Father Slattery himself had been a Games Master. The school later had a number of matches with another older School, Ahmadiya College. It was an ambitious venture for the school, in its first four years of existence on June 3rd 1960, to make its first attempt on the Zard Cup, a nationwide inter-Secondary School competition, which later became the Principals Cup. The school lost again to its counterpart institution, St. Gregory's College, 1-3. In 1961, it met the school again and lost 0-1 after an initial draw of 2-2. In 1962, Saint Finbarr's College won the Principals Cup for the first time, only six years after being established. This victory was repeated in 1966, 1968, and 1969. From then the team from Saint Finbarr's College became the team to beat. Weaker teams feared any match with Saint Finbarr's while stronger teams such as C.M.S. Grammar School, Baptist Academy, Igbobi College, and of course, the big brother Saint Gregory's College, always looked forward to a tough encounter. In 1971, 1972, and 1973, the school kept the Principals Cup, having won it three consecutive times.

It is noteworthy that in the 1970's and 1980's the school produced international players Thompson Oliha, Nduka Ugbade, Samson SiaSia, and Henry Nwosu, just to mention a few. In fact, in those days, for any candidate to aspire to come to St. Finbarr's, he had to be academically sound and/or physically superior in football. Stephen Keshi, who captained Finbarr's team, went on to be captain and coach of the national teams.

Rev. Father Denis J. Slattery placed a remarkably high premium on discipline and could expel any student even if he were the best in academics or in football if it were clear that he had committed a serious offense. The gate used to be referred to as the gate of no return. There was no point in appealing a case of expulsion. Father Slattery never entertained such appeals – no pleading, no begging, and no beseeching. Saint Finbarr's

College had four commandments, which constitute the Moral Pillars of the school.

(149)   Any student caught stealing will be expelled.

(150)   Any student caught copying during an examination will be expelled.

(151)   Any student caught leaving the school compound during school hours without the principal's permission will be expelled.

(152)   Any student caught smoking or with drugs will be expelled.

There were no in-between sanctions in the scale of punishment. You were either retained or expelled.

By the early 1970's Father Slattery had a vision of making St. Finbarr's College all-encompassing in technical studies. He decided to expand the technical workshops to cater both for the Senior and Junior Student. He introduced auto mechanics, electrical, and electronics departments. Two modern technical workshops were built from grants raised by his friends and overseas associates. The workshops were completed and fully equipped. They had hardly been used for two years when the government took over private schools in 1976. From 1976, the ideals for which Saint Finbarr's College was known, started to decline rapidly. Under government management, the school became overpopulated and student indiscipline reigned. The decline reached a frightening level in the second half of the 1990's.

Fortunately, the government eventually deemed it wise to officially relinquish the takeover of private schools on October 2nd, 2001. Thus, Saint Finbarr's College started its second phase of academic advancement, alas without the all-encompassing presence of Father Slattery. By the time the school was returned to the Church, Father Slattery had diverted his attention to other pastoral pursuits. The return of the school took effect in 2003, after much educational damage had been done by the government.

A furious academic cleansing ensued and many of the students who could not adjust were dismissed while those who could not stand the changes withdrew voluntarily. Consequently, by 2005, the enrollment at the school had gone down to a manageable level of 658 with the inherited "government students" constituting 413 students of the population. Below is a list of the noted principals of Saint Finbarr's College.

(1) Reverend Father Denis J. Slattery, Founding Principal, 1955-1975
(2) Anthony Omoera, 1975-1976
(3) Mr. A. A. Kpotie, 1977-1998
(4) Mr. Joseph Adusse, 1998-2001

The school has since been managed by a sequence of administrators from the Catholic Mission. Saint Finbarr's College has spread its positive influence around the world. Several "old boys" of the school are now in key productive and influential positions around the world. Like other notable high schools in Nigeria, Finbarr's has made significant contributions in human resource development in Nigeria. One distinct and unmistakable fact about Finbarr's is that it has a unifying force -- Rev. Fr. Denis Slattery (even after his death). The man and the name continue to strike a sense of refreshing chill in our hearts.

All graduates of Saint Finbarr's College remain immensely proud of the school's heritage. Father Slattery encouraged each person to embrace whatever his family religion dictated; but he demanded the study of the Bible as a source of well-rounded education. Thus, Biblical Religious Studies was a core subject at the school. Father taught his students to enjoy the thrills and perils of playing sports as preparation for the other challenges of life. The discipline received from the school served us very well. It is the single most crucial factor in the professional and personal success of Saint Finbarr's College "Old Boys." In the Yoruba language,

Finbarrians are fondly referred to as "Omo Slattery," meaning Slattery's children. He was our father both in the figurative and spiritual sense.

Father Slattery trained us to be who we are, and his lesson lives on in every one of us. Although his service was primarily in Nigeria, his good example should be publicized to serve other parts of the world. Every Finbarrian (former and present) has the unity of purpose to disseminate the glory of Saint Finbarr's College.

St. Finbarr's College was named after Saint Finbarr of Cork, Ireland. The narrative that follows is based partially on historical recollections of F. Ogundipe and supplemented by other student reports. The first stream of students in the college comprised 68 students in two classes of 34 students each. There were only four members of staff in the service of the school. Rev. Fr. Slattery the principal, two teachers and one office clerk who was a seminarian. Two weeks after resumption from January 21st-February 10th, the school went on recess on account of the visit of Queen of England and Head of Commonwealth of Nations, who was visiting Nigeria at the time. The whole class of 1956 took part in the events culminating in the Youth Day Parade in Lagos in honor of the Queen. St. Finbarr's College bore the parade number 162. Classes resumed in the middle of February. Father Slattery taught English Language, Literature, Religious Knowledge, and Latin. Mr. Bankole, now Chief Bankole, taught General Science and Arithmetic, Algebra Geometry and Singing. Mr. Ferdinand Ejike taught History and Geography. The first feast of Saint Finbarr, the patron saint of the school, was celebrated on September 25th, 1956 with Mass said by Father Slattery.

Early accounts by FFS members indicate that the first interhouse sports festival of the school took place in 1956. That same founding year, SFC participated in School Table Tennis Championships with Jamogha, Ayeni and Wilson as Finbarr's stars. The first soccer match was played against host primary school, St. Paul's Primary School. Finbarr's lost 1-2 in an exciting game, which featured Paul Gborjoh alias P J Cobbler. Toward the end of 1956 another encounter was organized with Babies Team of St. Gregory's College, a sister school from where Father Slattery came to found Finbarr's. In 1957, Finbarr's table tennis and soccer teams played the Leonians. Messrs Henry Ekpeti and Ayo Adefolaju and G U M Nwagbara joined the teaching staff. Mr. Ekpeti taught Latin, Mr. Adefolaju taught Mathematics, Nwagbara taught History and Geography, and Mr. Onabolu taught Fine Art. In 1958, Mr. Flyn joined the staff from Ireland to teach Physics and Chemistry. Mr. T C Nwosu, Mr. Oweh and Mr. Oguike also joined the teaching staff. In January 1959, students moved to the permanent site at Akoka. The Bursar was Pa Adefuye, Head Laborer Abu, Head of the new Department of Metalwork Mr. Mooney. Mr. Flynn assumed Headship of Woodwork Department. Mr. Tommy joined during that year to take over teaching of English Language and Literature from Father Slattery. Mr. Omopariola joined to teach History. From 1960 the complement of staff was enlarged to include Mr. Drumm for Additional Mathematics, Elementary Mathematics and Physics, Mr. Mackenzie for Chemistry, Mr. Omopariola for History, and Mr. Oguike for Geography. Mr. Oguike left that year for further studies in U.S. Mr. Nwagbara left the previous year but returned to teach History and Geogrpahy. Mr Nwosu left soon afterwards, and Biology fell into the laps of Mr. Okpara before Mr. Nwajei arrived.

Finbarr's entered the Grier Cup competition in 1960. That year, the only qualifier, Eddy Akika, won the coveted Victor Ludorum Trophy winning Hurdles, Long Jump and coming second in High Jump event. Finbarr's entered the Zard Cup on June 2nd, 1960, and lost to St. Gregory's College 1-3. Mr. Drumm was Games Master, Alex Tolefe was Team Manager and Finbarr's Captain was Albert Alotey. On the June 19th, 1961 Finbarr's lost once more to St. Gregory's 0-1 in quarter final of the cup. The same day, Finbarr's was eliminated from the National Table Tennis Championship at

Ibadan. Finbarr's lost at Semi Final Match 4-5 to Ansar U Deen College Isolo. Finbarr's stars were Heny Jamogha, Matin Adewusi, and Olusola John.

The first Zard Cup victory came in August 1962 when Finbarr's beat St. Gregory's College 2-1 after an earlier 2-2 draw under the captainship of Jide Akinosoye (Akinzawelle). It is vital to recall the following: Patrick Koshoni who designed SFC badge unofficially in November 1956 on the blackboard. A proper school badge came in 1957. Jaamogha created the current shape of the badge in 1957 and Father Slattery approved it.

The SFC van was purchased in 1959 and sprayed in school colors by Mr. Tommy. Ogundanna, a long-range runner was the first van driver.

As recollected by many graduates of SFC, tribes and tongues did not make any difference to anyone at Saint Finbarr's then, and they should not make any difference now. Other lists and accounts have been provided by sother Old Boys, including M. A. C. Odu. I did not try to reconcile the various lists of the First-Six students because, frankly, the lists are from different historical recollections and perspectives of the different early students and should be preserved as such. Even in the Bible, the Gospels by various Prophets are preserved as originally documented. In a non-computer era, all we can do is rely on the personal accounts and recollections of those offering testimonies. The government takeover of SFC led to the loss of crucial archival records of the early years of the college. Those records could have helped to authenticate each list.

After all these years, Saint Finbarr's College continues to excel in Academics, Sports, and Discipline. As of the time of this writing (2018), the school continues to receive accolades for its multi-dimensional accomplishments. In 2017, Business Day Research and Intelligence Unit (BRIU) published a guide to the best schools in Lagos, Nigeria. Saint Finbarr's College was listed among the topmost secondary schools in Lagos State. The school's performance in the West African Senior School Certificate Examinations since 2013 have been extraordinary. Based on the number of students who obtained five credits including Mathematics and English Language, the pass rates have been 98.7% in 2013, 100% in 2014, 97.4% in 2015 95%, in 2016 97.4% and 98.2% in 2017. Finbarr's students have won laurels at various academic competitions, including Helmbridge, Olympiad, Inter-collegiate Quiz and Debate, and so on.

Please score a checkmark for academics!

In the same vein, Saint Finbarr's College won Soccer Guarantee Trust (GT) Bank Championship on June 29th, 2017 at Onikan Stadium, Lagos, Nigeria. The school has expanded its sports excellence to include basketball, tennis, volleyball, and badminton.

Please score a checkmark for sports excellence!

Overall, the virtues of discipline, self-control, respect, care for others, honesty, obedience, hard work, dedication, diligence, and resilience continue to be instilled in Finbarr's students daily. Thus, Saint Finbarr's College provides holistic education for its students.

In an era when holy men are charged with doing unholy things, Father Slattery was holy and dedicated to the cause throughout his life of sanctity. There was no flattery or fakery about him.

"Slattery, No Flattery" was a common catchphrase in Lagos, Nigeria about the ways and deeds of Father Slattery. A picture is worth a thousand words. There are not enough words to describe the immense widespread contributions of Reverend Denis Joseph Slattery to education in Nigeria. So, I have generously supplemented words with photographic images of the deeds of Father Slattery. Even after his death since 2003, his deeds continue to influence the lives of those who ever had the good fortune to be associated with Father Slattery either directly or through the continuing legacy of his Saint Finbarr's College, Akoka-Yaba, Lagos, Nigeria.

In the days of Father Slattery, all roads led to Saint Finbarr's College. Parents in Lagos wished and clamored for their children to attend Saint Finbarr's, even though there were several other highly regarded secondary schools in Lagos. These schools included King's College, Igbobi College, Saint Gregory's College, Ansa-ud-deen College, and Baptist Academy. As a high school aspirant in those days, my initial goal was to attend King's College, until I came across the educational and sports triumphs of Saint Finbarr's College and the personal and direct touch of Father Slattery. It was a dichotomy of a special kind to have a school that excelled in sports while simultaneously winning national accolades in educational accomplishments. I was provisionally selected for an interview to enter King's College, but utterly devastated when I did not make the cut. By divine intervention, I was admitted to Saint Finbarr's College. The story of my admission to Saint Finbarr's is still a fortuitous occurrence that still astonishes me even today. I am convinced that I would not have been any more competitive in 1969 than I was in 1968 in entering a reputable high school in Lagos area. The positive experience of how Saint Finbarr's College came to my academic rescue still determines how I view educational opportunities these days and how I fervently support giving educational opportunities to qualified young minds of today.

Reverend Father Joseph Slattery was a product of a strong Irish heritage. The Irish are noted for their constant search for self-determination among dominant neighbors. He later became a Catholic priest, founder of Schools, sport administrator, editor, and journalist. Father Slattery is a leap-year child, and he was always proud of this, claiming to be only one-fourth of his actual age. His parents, Mr. Timothy Slattery, and Mrs. Kate Slattery were blessed with eight children. Denis was the seventh child of the family.

Timothy Slattery was a master-cutter and Kate Slattery was a trained dressmaker. They were both from Barrington, Fermoy, a provincial town in Cork, in south Ireland, where the Slattery generations had lived since the 13th century.

The Slattery family was known as "Doers," a family with a deep sense of adventure, enterprise, and great achievement. The Irish adventurous spirit has remained their greatest contribution to the world. They stride the world in pastoral and political life, breaking new grounds in all spheres.

Many people today remember the Irish as the descendants of the builders of Modern America. In 1776, at the signing of the American Constitution, six Irish citizens were signatories to that historic moment. Timothy Slattery was disciplinarian, stern, and straight. Kate Slattery was quiet, serene, and charitable– a combination that was perhaps very necessary for raising eight children.

The Slattery's were a family of athletes, a trait taken from their father. Timothy Slattery was a great footballer and represented his country as a potential athlete. His children, particularly Denis, simply continued the tradition. At a tender age, Denis J. Slattery was enrolled for his kindergarten education at the Christian Brothers School in Fermoy. He was the only Slattery who did not attend the local Convent school. Young Denis refused to go "to the nuns" at the Presentation Convent. At the Christian Brothers School, the young Slattery was remembered as a wild young man. A healthy kind of wildness, they would say. His activities included *"climbing the highest tree over the River Blackwater and plunging into the deepest depth, searching the woods and forest for birds' nests and eggs, and following the grey hounds on Sunday Soccer."*

He became an Altar boy at the age of ten. He was an excellent liturgist but an average Altar boy. Once an old man who was regular at Mass called him and said, "You serve Mass beautifully. I think you will make a priest." This harmless remark would come to plant the seed of his vocation. Young Denis had a seriousness of purpose and had often talked about vocations and in time, he entered Junior Secondary.

In the Seminary, life was drab and hard. Food was poor, dormitories were badly heated, and the chapel was only heated on Sundays. By the second year he had sciatica. He recovered and buried himself deeper into his chosen vocation. He spent two years in the seminary. The extra year was spent receiving private tutoring lessons in Latin to enable him to pass the Matriculation examination.

1932 marked when Denis Joseph Slattery began his missionary vocation. By 1934, he entered the Novitiate in Clough for a period of two years, and on the December 17th,1939, he was ordained a priest. He was studious and prayerful at the Seminary, so he was chosen to go to Rome and study the scriptures in 1940. He was not destined to be in Rome, which was made clear when the second World War broke out.

Father Slattery's first assignment after ordainment was to contribute to raising money for the Church. He was humiliated because he had to beg. Little did he know that he would be doing the same for the rest of his life. This was the beginning of an arduous and tasking pastoral life. In Lagos, Nigeria, Archbishop Leo Taylor was in dire need of teachers for his diocese. In 1941, the World War II was at its peak. Rev. Fr. Denis Joseph Slattery, 25-year-old Catholic Priest of the Society of African Missions (SMA), was on his way to his posting in Africa. This young priest was part of a growing Irish spiritual empire that included China and the Philippines. The trip was punctuated by a German air attack on the convoy. A German plane had dropped three bombs on their ship, which was sailing from Glasgow in a convoy of fifty ships carrying Allied Forces on the Atlantic Ocean. In the tremor following the bombing, the ship rocked violently, dipping from left to right, but did not sink. When they finally arrived in Lagos, the Germans were bombing the Lagos port and ships were not berthing. The ship redirected to Port-Harcourt where she berthed. The journey was continued by train from Port-Harcourt to Kaduna and then Lagos.

In 1941, Lagos had its fascination for the young Irishman. He did not reckon with Ilawe-Ekiti, a village in the hinterland of the Western part of Nigeria. Archbishop Taylor was waiting in Lagos. He would welcome the young priest and send him to Ilawe-Ekiti. On his first night at Ilawe-Ekiti, Fr. Slattery was confronted by a strange pastoral duty. At midnight, a black face had poked its head into the house to ask the Rev. Father to come immediately and give blessing to a dying Christian. He performed his pastoral duties, but the picture remained with him, the black face and the black night.

By the 1940s Archbishop Leo Taylor had built a strong missionary base in the Lagos Diocese. Well-respected and loved by many, Archbishop Taylor was a member of the Society of African Missions (SMA) and of course, the quintessential missionary. He called Rev. Fr. Slattery to Lagos in 1942. At this point, the young priest he sent to Ilawe-Ekiti spoke the Yoruba language and could give confession in the language. In Lagos, he was posted to St. Gregory's College, Obalende, as a teacher and games master. His stature seemed to have endeared him to his new students. A mutual relationship was formed which led to great exploits on the football field. His stay at St. Gregory's College was short.

In 1943, he was posted to the Catholic Printing Press as journalist and later Editor of *Catholic Herald*. At the Herald he cultivated a radical posture and became concerned about Nigeria's self-determination as he thundered from the newspaper and the pulpit, "Nigeria for Nigerians." His years as Editor of the Catholic Herald were turbulent. Through the paper, he contributed to the pre-independence struggle, forming a lasting relationship with Labor

leaders and politicians. He used the Herald to champion the workers'
cause during the general strike of 1945 and the Enugu Coal Mine strike
where twenty striking miners were killed. Thrice, the British Colonial
Government tried to throw him out of the country, after several warnings.
According to him he was just doing his duty. *"The British are gone, and I
(Slattery) am still here,"* Slattery would later boast. Fr. Slattery later went
on to write his master's thesis on the labor struggle in Nigeria. A founding
member of the Nigerian Union of Journalists (NUJ) and the Guild of
Editors, Fr. Slattery contributed immensely to labor and journalism.

Also, during these years, he made remarkable contributions to the
development of football and football administration in Nigeria. As an
inside-left, he had played first division football in Lagos with Lagos United.
It was as a referee that he made his greatest contribution. His Excellency,
Nnamdi Azikiwe, first President of the Federal Republic of Nigeria, was
Slattery's linesman in those days. He recalls that he made great strides
as a referee probably because he was a Catholic priest; therefore, he
was presumed honest. Rev. Fr. Denis Slattery was, at various times, the
Chairman of the Referees' Association, Executive member of the Lagos
Amateur Football Association, and Chairman of the Nigerian Football
Association (N.F.A.)

In 1956, Archbishop Taylor invited Fr. Denis Slattery to establish a secondary
school in Lagos. Fr. Slattery saw this assignment as an opportunity to
contribute to society as an educationist and a sports administrator. Thus,
in January 1956, he founded St. Finbarr's College as a Technical Grammar
School. Classes started on the premises of St. Paul's Primary School in
Ebute Metta. St. Finbarr's College became the first school in Nigeria to
run in duality a Technical and Grammar School. This was an innovation
that endeared the school to parents. Fr. Slattery chose to name the school
after Saint Finbarr, a great educator, a priest, and a bishop who founded a
monastery of prayer and an institution.

In 1960, the school was approved by the Ministry of Education. By this singular action St. Finbarr's College became eligible to participate in the prestigious schoolboy football competition, the Principal Cup. This had a special thrill for Rev. Fr. Slattery. He had one burning ambition since the day he founded St. Finbarr's College -- to win the prestigious Principal Cup! The name, St. Finbarr's College, was to become synonymous with schoolboy soccer and academic excellence in Nigeria.

Having moved from the premises of St. Paul's Primary School to its permanent site in Akoka in 1959, St. Finbarr's College made its debut in the Principal Cup in 1960. They lost to St. Gregory's College that year and in 1961. In 1962, St. Finbarr's College won the Principal Cup. This was the beginning of unprecedented soccer supremacy in schoolboy football. The college went on to win the Principal Cup for a record nine times. The secret of this success was physical fitness, the provision of necessary training equipment, and a standard pitch. The myth claims that if Fr. Slattery coached the Nigerian national side of those days, they would have won the World Cup. Today, some of his concepts on football administration remain valid.

Football was the delight of the students of St. Finbarr's and Fr. Slattery succeeded in pushing for excellence in other sporting endeavors. In 1960, the College made its debut in the Grier Cup. That year, Eddy Akika of St. Finbarr's College took the coveted Victor Ludorum Trophy winning first in the Hurdles, Long Jump, and second in the High Jump event.

Slattery ensured that sporting excellence was clearly tied to academic excellence. Through the years and on many occasions, the College had the enviable record of scoring a 100% pass in the WAEC entries. Thus, students of St. Finbarr's were noted for hard work and hard play. Today, Saint Finbarr's College has produced numerous Nigerians who got to the peak of their professional careers and contributed significantly to the development of the Nation. Notable amongst them are: Vice-Admiral

Patrick Koshoni (Rtd.), Major-General Cyril Iweze, Nze Mark Odu, Otunba Anthony Olusegun Odugbesan, Dr. J. A. Ikem, Dr. Segun Ogundimu, Chief Empire Kanu P, Professor Steve Elesha, Dr. Tayo Shokunbi, Airvice Marshal Wilfred Ozah, Tom Borha, Segun Ajanlekoko.

Father Denis Slattery retired from St. Finbarr's College in 1975. He returned to his first love, his pastoral duties. He returned to St. Denis Catholic Church, Bariga and provided service to the Church as Parish priest. He eventually retired as Vicar-General to the Archdiocese of Lagos and left his footprints in the sand of time. Rev. Fr. Denis J. Slattery is a true Nigerian patriot of Irish parentage, who contributed to the pioneering of technical education in secondary schools and the growth of football administration in Nigeria. Rev. Fr. D. J. Slattery was a Missionary, Educationist, Journalist, Technocrat, Football Administrator, a mentor of sports, and one of nature's exceptional gentlemen.

Rev. Father Slattery was an outstanding example of the Irish Catholic Missionary movement, which in this century saw many thousands of Irish Reverend Fathers and Sisters leave Ireland to take the Christian message to the four corners of the world. He dedicated 56 years of his earthly life to the development of the Nigerian humanity. A keen athlete and journalist, he served Nigeria in many capacities including Chairmanship of the Nigerian Football Association (NFA). He brought with him from Ireland, a keen appreciation of the value of education, without which freedom, responsibility, or development is impossible. In his great desire to inform, Father Slattery became actively involved in the development of Journalism and Education. His major contribution to education, St. Finbarr's College, is named after Saint Finbarr – the patron saint of his native county of Cork. His other enduring legacy to Nigeria, football, comes from his own enthusiastic love of sport. Here, he obviously tapped into a rich vein in Nigerian life – a truly fanatical love of football. A list of his achievements and contributions is presented below.

SLATTERY'S ACHIEVEMENTS AND CONTRIBUTIONS

1. Vice-Chairman of the Society for the Bribe Scorners
2. Assistant Honorary Secretary of the Nigerian Olympic & British Empire Games Association
3. Publicity Secretary of the Lagos District Amateur Football Association
4. Member of the Council of African Students in North America
5. Assistant Secretary of the Nigerian Football Association
6. Honorary Secretary of the Commonwealth Games Appeal Fund
7. Catholic Representative of the Broadcasting Services (Religious)
8. Chairman of the Nigerian Referees Association
9. Chairman of the Council of Social Workers (Boy Scouts, Catholic Youth Organization, Salvation Army, Boys' Brigade, Y.M.C.A., Colony Welfare Organizations, Girls Guide, and Youth Clubs)
10. Chairman of the Leper Colony of Nigeria
11. Chairman of the Nigerian Football Association (NFA)
12. Editor of the Catholic Herald (Newspaper)
13. Foundation Member of the Nigerian Union of Journalists
14. Member of the Nigerian Guild of Editors
15. Founder and Principal of St. Finbarr's College, Akoka, Lagos
16. Founder of SS Peter & Paul, Shomolu
17. Founder of Our Lady of Fatima Private School, Bariga
18. Founder of St. Joseph's Vocational School, Akoka
19. Coordinator of the T.I.M.E. Project, Akoka
20. Founder of St. Finbarr's Catholic Church, Akoka, Lagos
21. Founder of St. Gabriel's Catholic Church
22. Founder of St. Flavius Catholic Church, Oworonshoki
23. Parish Priest of St. Denis Catholic Church
24. Vicar-General of the Catholic Church of Nigeria – Lagos Archdiocese (Rtd.)

Selected Quotes from Father Slattery's Book, *My Life Story*, West African Book Publishers, Limited, Ilupeju, Lagos, Nigeria, 1996.

Before his death, SFCOBA beseeched Father Slattery to give us his own account of the recollection of Saint Finbarr's College in the early days. Below what he told us:

"The Queen of England visited Nigeria during one of those years. When I bowed and shook hands with the Queen, I was quickly passed on to the duke. The Queen took much more notice of the ladies in the line. The duke knew about my association with Football and refereeing. In the short conversation we had he made a very profound statement that I often used afterwards with an air of pride. The Duke of Edinburgh said to me, "Football is as good as its referee. A bad referee can spoil Soccer."

"But what has happened to our beloved country, one of the richest gems of Africa? What has become of all our dreams? How many have paid the supreme price sacrificing their lives at home and in foreign lands to build a new Nigeria? Thousands died in Egypt, North Africa, Burma, etc."

"Look at Nigeria today, several years after independence. Today, sad to say, Nigeria is riddled with corruption from the top to the bottom. No segment of Nigerian Society is free from the Cankerworm of bribery that has eaten into the bowels of our nation."

"As a result of a lecture I gave one time when I blamed the budding political leaders that they had fallen very quickly for the flesh pots offered by the Colonialists by taking huge salaries as ministers with or without portfolios, (I stated that there was no Freedom in Nigeria but our neo-political leaders were dancing to the tune of the British overlords), the next day, I was on the receiving end of a few scathing remarks in the press.

One paper wrote, "Father Slattery must have been drugged or drunk. He could not see wood or the trees!!"

But another paper replied, "Father Slattery is destined to be the 'Cardinal Minzenty' of Hungary to be sacrificed on the altar of British imperialism." I was neither. I was Catholic Priest that stood for freedom – freedom to worship the true God and to enjoy the good things of life."

"I always regarded the visit to the Holy Land as a gift from my people in Nigeria. Had I not come to Nigeria in the first place, I would not have ever visited those sacred places that are particularly dear to the Catholic Priest.

Thank you, Nigeria, for this wonderful gift on my 11th birthday, when I turned 44 years old. Don't forget that I am a Leap Year Child."

The Four Commandments of St. Finbarr's in Slattery's Time:

"There were "Four Commandments", not ten, strictly implemented to help maintain discipline. Any student violating these rules went down that "Corridor of no return." This had become a catch phrase in the school. These were the commandments:

Any student caught stealing will be expelled.

Any student caught copying at examination time will be expelled. Any student that fails is automatically expelled. He is not allowed to Repeat.

Any student leaving the compound during school hours without the principal's permission will be expelled.

Any student caught smoking or with drugs will be expelled.

These were often discussed as the moral pillars of St. Finbarr's College, and the key to our policy. Proved beyond a shadow of doubt after thorough investigation, there was no mercy shown, even to a Form 1 Boy if caught breaking these decrees."

Everything about Father Slattery was for real and no lottery. He never sought fame and accolades. His approach was based on resolute pursuit rather than a game-of-chance undertaking. He pursued and did everything with resolute and unwavering commitment. He called each thing as he saw it. He was not a man of narrative pontification. He got to the point and that was it.

To further appreciate my story, the reader must understand the background of Rev. Fr. Denis Slattery, the Irish priest who touched the lives of many Nigerians. He was an exceptional human being from the time he was born until his death.

In a 1996 newspaper editorial, writer Ochereome Nnanna presented an accurate characterization of Father Slattery on his eightieth birthday as a man of no flattery. A true renaissance man, Father Slattery said it as he saw it. All the accolades that Father Slattery had received over the years, both while he was alive and following his death, contain the same unmistakable fact. There was never any flattery about him. He was a man of no pretensions. What you saw was what you got from him. I have tried to pattern myself after him in that regard. A friend once called me "Deji of no pretensions." I still cherish that characterization.

Father Slattery prided himself as an Irish-Nigerian and has been credited with many contributions to the development of modern Nigeria (both pre-independence and following independence). He was a patriot to the core, an activist for righteousness not only from the standpoint of religion, but also from the points of social equality and political self-determination.

His 1996 Memoirs, **My Life Story**, published by West African Book Publishers, Ltd. gives an incredibly detailed account of his contributions to Nigeria and Nigerians.

One admirable attribute of his work in Nigeria was his commitment to a non-parochial view of issues. He supported the views of different religious leanings, if the views matched the tenets of good citizenship. There was tolerance of religion and economic status at St. Finbarr's. Similarly, there was complete tribal and ethnic harmony at the school because Father Slattery saw to it that everyone accepted everyone else.

As Principal of Saint Finbarr's College, Father Slattery used the threat of being expelled as a deterrent to discourage unruly behavior. His common warning was "I will send you down that dirt road, and you will never come back, and God is my witness" He, of course, was referring to a one-way journey down the narrow dirt road of Akoka. Saint Finbarr's College campus was the one building in that area of Akoka at that time. It was a long dusty hike from the Unilag Road to the school with heavy bushes on either side of the road.

Father Slattery was a man of small stature, but his heart, energy, and enthusiasm matched those of a giant. He put his energetic temperament to effective use in chasing misbehaving students around the school compound. With his robe flowing wildly in the wind, he would take off after boys that he suspected were contravening school rules. It was a game of cat and mouse. He monitored the school premises himself. Latecomers and those sneaking out of the school compound during the day hardly escaped his roving eyes. He could run, jump, and tackle ruffian boys. He was a multi-faceted principal and we all admired, revered, and feared him all at the same time. He also prided himself on being a boxer. Whether he was ever a boxer, or whether he put on that bluff to keep us in line, was a frequent debate among the students. When angered, he would challenge the students to a fistfight. Of course, he knew none of us would dare take him on, and he capitalized on that fact. Secondary school kids were much older in those days. We had classmates who were in their early twenties. However, none was big or man enough to confront the wrath of Father Slattery.

"Father is coming" was a frequent look-out call from boys doing what they were not supposed to be doing. Just like prairie dogs scenting an approaching predator, the boys would run in different directions. There would often be one unfortunate boy that would be chased down by Father. He would drag the boy into the principal's office for an appropriate punishment. At the next school assembly, we would all hear about the latest mischievous acts of "a few bad boys." Father Slattery enjoyed those encounters to get his exercise to keep fit and trim. He was a nurturing disciplinarian. As strict as he was, Father Slattery was also a very forgiving individual. One minute he was shouting and ranting about something, the next minute he was patting you on the back for a good academic or football performance.

How he found the time, resolve, and energy to do all that he did was beyond explanation. Those of us who have tried to emulate his ways can usually be identified by our diverse interests both in avocation and recreation. Father Slattery was a very effervescent man; always excited and animated about everything. There was never a dull moment with him around

REFERENCES FOR CHAPTER TWO

Slattery, Denis J. (1996), **My Life Story**, West African Book Publishers, Limited, Ilupeju, Lagos, Nigeria, 1996.

CHAPTER 3

MY TIME AT FINBARR'S: ACADEMICS AND DISCIPLINE

Although I had rudimentary soccer skills from neighborhood games at Ebute-Metta, I did not have the skills to qualify for the high sports standards of Finbarr's. However, that was not a problem. Academics also opened the door of Finbarr's. Coupling incoming academics with discipline can ensure success at the end of the day. Getting into Saint Finbarr's College in 1968 paved the way for my eventual academic pathway, professional path, and career advancement. To understand how Saint Finbarr's College transformed my life, one needs to know my own beginning and early years and how I came to cross paths with Rev. Fr. Slattery. I overcame several educational adversities before reaching my present educational attainment. Glory be to the Good Lord.

I was born on September 2nd, 1952, into the Sharafa Ola Badiru Onisarotu family of Epe, Lagos State. By the standard of the day, it was an affluent family. My father was a building contractor and traveled extensively in pursuit of his profession. Several of his children were born outside of Epe. He was a particularly popular person at Okegbogi Street in Ondo township in the late 1940s and early 1950s. I was only five years old when my father died on April 12th, 1958. Thus, began the family hiatus that would disrupt what would have otherwise been a steady and sheltered upbringing. We were unprepared for his sudden death, and our family did not know how to manage and care for the younger children in the large family.

Fortunately, there were older children among us at that time. The adults in the family "distributed" the younger ones among themselves to see to their upbringing. In the process, I was shuttled from one place to another, from one sibling to another, and from one extended relative to another. Over a period of a few years, I stayed with brothers, sisters, uncles, and some distant relatives. I had the good fortune of having a large and extended family with no shortage of good Samaritans willing to take me on as a ward.

The result of being a migrant ward was that I could not start school until 1961 --- at the late age of nine! I started elementary school at Zumratul Islamiyyah Elementary school in the heart of Lagos in 1961. My first encounter with counting and reciting the alphabet was not until I was nine years old. This late start, coupled with the fact that I started school in Lagos, where primary education was for eight years (in those days) compared to six years in the Western region, meant that I was five years behind my educational cohorts. One thing that was in my favor at that time was my maturity level. At that age, I already understood the importance of education. I did not need any prodding or forcing to go to school. My level of maturity made me more attentive and appreciative of the teachers in the classroom, so I was able to take in all lessons presented by the teachers. I did not need any supplementary lessons outside of school. In those days, teachers and observers erroneously attributed my excellent school performance to my higher level of intelligence. For a long time, I mistakenly believed it too. What was fueling my academic performance was my high maturity level. I enjoyed excellent rapport with my classmates and teachers. I could tell that the teachers not only liked me, but also respected me. For this reason, I never got into any punishment episode at school. I went through elementary school without ever being punished at school, in an age when school punishment was very rampant. The same record was later repeated throughout my secondary school years.

I suffered enough punishment at the homes of my guardians for disobeying them to make up for the grace that I enjoyed at school. Contrary to the typical situation in those days, school was my refuge. I enjoyed going to school to escape what I considered to be a very oppressive disciplinary home environment. It happened that, as a child, what I considered to be oppressive chores at home turned out to be valuable lessons that continue to serve me well at home until today. I remain very handy at home, particularly in the kitchen and general household chores. My adoption of school as a refuge was fortuitous because it paved the way for my sound academic foundation. I knew I would not be able to study at home, so I paid every bit of attention to the lectures at school. That way, I imbibed everything the teacher had to say. I never had an opportunity for supplementary lessons or studying at home. I relied entirely on school lectures. I could not afford to not pay attention at school. Children nowadays have the luxury of private lessons. Sometimes they get too lackadaisical about the opportunities.

In those days, I had a free-wheeling lifestyle of freedom to roam the neighborhood streets in search of fun. This did not sit well with my guardians, who preferred for me to be indoors to perform household chores. I was frequently on a collision course with my guardians about my over-commitment to playing around the neighborhood. Despite this, I still enjoyed good relationships with my guardians primarily because I performed well in school. I recall an elderly neighbor intervening and pleading with one of my guardians to spare me a punishment on account of my school performance. He opined that, despite my playing too much, I was still doing very well at school compared to my playmates, who were playing and not doing well at school.

One of my favorite guardians was my uncle, the late Chief Alao Shabi. I learnt a lot of calm demeanor and rationality speaking with him. Although he punished me a few times also, it was always at the instigation of unfair reports getting to him about what and what offense I had committed. Typical reports were about my being seen riding a bicycle around the neighborhood, swimming in a local public pool, or playing football on the playground. These were all considered dangerous and unauthorized acts in those days. That some of us learnt to ride bicycles, swim, and play football was a credit to our mischievous acts of running away from home for a few hours to engage in these fun but "dangerous" acts. My uncle was a scrap-metal dealer. He had a scrap-metal shop at Idumagbo in the heart of Lagos in the 1960s. His shop was later moved to Owode Onirin in the outskirts of Lagos. From 1965 through 1967, I helped him tend the scrap metal shop along with his Hausa assistant, named Gaji. The general expectation was that after elementary school, I would become a full-time apprentice to my uncle and eventually go into the scrap metal business, which was a lucrative business in those days. My uncle engaged in exporting scrap metals overseas. He interacted with white expatriates through the ports at Apapa. The decades following Nigeria's independence saw a decline in the lucrative level of scrap metals. If I had gone into that business, I would be mired in the economic depression associated with it now.

I learnt a lot of direct activities from Gaji. He introduced me to the properties of various metals and how to manage them. He gave me an early (albeit unscientific) appreciation for various metals. We sorted scrap metals into their respective categories. We dealt with mercury, silver, iron, steel, copper, brass, platinum, and other metals. I do not recall handling gold in those days. The direct skills still serve me well today in handling household tools. Even now, my most cherished possessions are the implements of household work such as hammers, pliers, screw drivers, and drills. Anyone visiting my home now can hardly miss my intimate relationships with these implements.

I graduated from elementary school in 1967 and was supposed to enter secondary school in January 1968. Due to my excellent academic performance and excellent result in the common entrance examination, it was believed that I would not encounter any difficulty in gaining admission into a secondary school. However, there were other obstacles lurking beneath the raw academic record. What I thought should not matter in gaining admission into a reputable school were actually major obstacles in the eyes of the secondary school officials.

The prospect of not being able to pay school fees prevented my admission to the most reputable secondary schools. My sister, the late Mrs. Omowunmi Ayodele Durosimi (previously Mrs. Shojobi), insisted that I must go to a reputable high school because of her belief and confidence in my academic promise. She had monitored my performance throughout my elementary school and concluded that nothing, but the best schools were appropriate for me. She had attended Queens School, Ede, in the Western Region. She had the vision of my attending schools such as Kings College, Government College, and other well-known schools. I applied to all those schools. Based on my common entrance examination results, I was invited for interviews at all the schools. I was self-assured and confident about my academic-related performance at the interviews. However, I was naïve about the other factors that were considered in admitting children to those schools. Frequently, at those interviews, I had no shoes on and wore simple clothes. I attended the interviews by myself. No accompanying parents, siblings, or relatives. If I had asked my family members, I could have received appropriate support to put on an "air" of being well-off enough to attend the schools. I made a deliberate and conscious decision to attend the interview just as I was – without any pretensions. I was somehow arrogant about my academic capabilities, and I believed the school authorities would be impressed. I was very wrong. My attitude going into the interviews was that I wanted to challenge the interviewers to ask me any question about school subjects so that I could impress them with my knowledge.

Very often, however, questions were raised only about tangential elements that had nothing to do with school subjects. Typical questions that I was asked were:

> *Who will pay your school fees?*
> *Where is your father's house?*
> *Did your mother attend secondary school?*
> *Has anybody in your family attended this school?*
> *Is your mother a trader or a government worker?*
> *What is your professional goal?*
> *Which elementary school did you attend?*
> *Have you ever attended a nursery school?*

The interviewers thought I would be a misfit at an Ivy-League type of secondary school. Although Zumratul Islamiyyah Elementary School was a good school on the inside, it was not highly regarded externally. This could be because it was in the rough inner-city part of Lagos. Its location was noted more for commercial activities rather than as an academic base for a well-regarded school. The school has since been demolished and the site is designated for other commercial purposes.

I had no doubt the other kids had been well-coached about the interview questions and had well-honed answers for all such silly questions. I was brash and determined not to stoop too low as to give answers that would amount to pretensions. My sister had expected that many schools would be so impressed with my academic performance that they would admit me with scholarship offers. There was no prior arrangement or preparation by my family regarding how to pay my school fees. My sister was caught off guard by the disappointing admission outcomes.

To be fair, my older age played against me. There I was, trying to enter secondary school at the ripe age of sixteen. I was five years older than my contemporary's seeking admission at the same time. Not knowing my history of starting school late, the interviewers equated my advanced age to low intelligence in elementary school. Their natural suspicion of my being academically dim did not match the documented performance on paper. So, they decided to err on the side of caution.

Zumratul did not have a secondary school at that time. Otherwise, I would have been a sure winner to progress from Zumratul Elementary School to Zumratul Secondary School. I was like a goldfish out of a backyard pond looking to be placed in an ivy-league aquarium.

My attendance at Zumratul Elementary School had been by accident rather than by design. At the age of nine years in 1961, elementary schools were reluctant to enroll me. I was a raw and untested pupil with no prior preparation to enter school. The "raw" part of me at that time was what led to my moniker of "BB Raw-Raw" later. BB stands for my middle and last names -- Bodunde Badiru. I proudly autographed that insignia on my early drawings and paintings. The full salutation was "BB Raw-Raw, Broken Bottle Never Tires," whatever that was supposed to mean, I never knew. Many of my early friends still call me BB; but most people have forgotten or never knew of the Raw-Raw part of the motto.

In the search for my first elementary school, it happened that a sister-in-law, the late Mrs. Shadiyat Badiru, wife of my late brother, Mr. Atanda Badiru, was a book seller at the school at the time that an elementary school was being sought for me. She took me to the principal, who queried me about why I was just entering school for the first time. I was able to give him satisfactory answers because I was old enough to be cognizant of my situation and the consequences of my predicament. The principal was impressed with my mature communication abilities. He decided to enroll me, jokingly making a comment that "Enu e dun," which satirically meant that my stories were tantalizing.

In 1967, I was invited to several Secondary School admission interviews. Notable among these were King's College, Lagos and Government College, Ibadan. None of these were successful. Even though the interview experiences were not successful, they were, nonetheless, very gratifying. The honor of being invited to interview at those schools brought much pride and joy to the officials of my elementary school. The interview at Government College was a protracted one-week affair that culminated in written and oral tests on various subjects. I was informed that I did very well on the tests but did not meet the cut-off requirements in the overall interview. I returned to Lagos empty-handed.

After attending several interviews with no success, I concluded that I needed a better answer to the question of "Who will pay your school fees?" I embarked on an effort to seek financial support from local philanthropists. One noted person that I appealed to was the late Chief S. B. Bakare. I had heard of several philanthropic projects that he had undertaken. I was hopeful that he would be so impressed by my academic potential that he might want to invest in my education. I crafted a well-written letter to him explaining my plight. The letter included carefully composed paragraphs that would indicate to him my knowledge and command of the English language, even at that age. I included statements about my common entrance exam results. I never received a response.

My disappointment was contained only by the prospects of contacting other philanthropists in Lagos. There was no shortage of such benefactors in Lagos in those days. Unfortunately, none of them came my way. All my attempts at pursuing philanthropic grace were futile. Years later, I began to understand why I might not have heard from those that I contacted. It could have been that they never received my letters at all because I did not have the correct addresses. It could also have been that their administrative assistants obstructed the delivery of the letters. They received thousands of requests, beyond what they could comfortably respond to or provide financial assistance for.

My admission to Saint Finbarr's College was nothing short of a miracle that manifested itself through the hands of Father Slattery. After several months searching for a secondary school without success, my family's attention turned to exploring other options for my future. There were discussions about me going into some trade apprenticeship. A popular option was for me to capitalize on my drawing skills by going into a sign-writing business. Imagine the caption, "BB Raw-Raw Signs" or "BB, the Sign Writer" on a roadside kiosk.

Saint Finbarr's College was considered an option due to a fortunate act of geographical proximity. I was living with my sister at the University of Lagos Staff Quarters at that time. She was married to Dr. Wole Shojobi, who was a Civil Engineering lecturer at the University. Having found no school yet, my sister decided that we should consider one of the local schools on the mainland of Lagos. Thus, Saint Finbarr's College came into the picture. Being in the immediate vicinity of Unilag, Finbarr's was a convenient choice.

The school was appealing because it was nearby and did not have a boarding school. Attending a boarding school far away would have compounded my financial inability to pay the school fees. My sister contacted Saint Finbarr's College and found out that there might be openings in the school. It was already two weeks after school session started in January 1968. The fact that openings existed at that time was a fortuitous coincidence. The school was looking for a few additional diligent students and I was looking for a good school. My sister sent me to the school to inquire. As usual, I went to the school all by myself.

It was a good thing Father Slattery did not care what a prospective student looked like. I went to school without shoes and no impressive clothing. Unlike my previous secondary school interview experiences, Father Slattery addressed me the same way he addressed all the parents who had come to the school with their kids to inquire about the "rumored" openings. Father was quite an impressive and blessed being. Although it was the first time that I would speak directly to a white man, I completely understood him, and he understood me. This is a credit to his years of living in Nigeria and communicating with various categories of Nigerians in local communities. He announced to everyone that there were **only three** vacancies. He cautioned that no parent should approach him to lobby for the open positions. He was going to fill the three vacancies purely based on merit. There were several parents and kids in the audience when the announcement was made. I was the only unaccompanied boy in the group. By my own estimate, there must have been at least two hundred boys. I concluded that I had no chance and presumed this to be another disappointing outcome in my lengthy and lonely search for a secondary school.

How was Father Slattery going to ensure a fair process of selecting only three kids from the hundreds that were interested in being admitted? He laughed at the parents' inquiry. He responded that he had an ingenious plan. He told everyone to come back on a specified date. He did not say what the selection plan was. He kept the plan secret to prevent any attempt by any parent to usurp the process. Without knowing the selection process, no one knew how to prepare or scheme for success. He told everyone there was no need for the kids to prepare anything for the appointed date. Just show up on time. Disappointed, everyone left for that day. I was filled with misgivings about the whole thing. I was heartened by the fact that I was still in the running.

On the appointed day, I showed up at the school, unaccompanied, as usual. Father Slattery told everyone to assemble in the open field across from the Assembly Hall. There were hundreds of anxious eyes. There were murmurings among the parents regarding what was going on and what was going to happen. Father Slattery stepped onto the high concrete pavement bordering the Assembly Hall. This position gave him an elevated view of the audience. It was like being on a high-rise podium. After positioning himself majestically in front of and above the audience, he announced that he was going to select three kids from the audience to fill the open vacancies based on the common entrance exam results. Everyone was baffled. How was he going to do that? Father asked two clerks from the school office to come onto the pavement. A table and a chair were hurriedly positioned on the pavement. The clerks had been inside the Assembly Hall, waiting for Father's instruction to emerge. After the clerks were settled, with one sitting on the chair and the other standing beside the table with papers and pencils in hand, Father Slattery beckoned to the school secretary to bring out a big pile of typed sheets. The pile must have measured almost one foot above the table. People in the audience looked at one another anxiously. No one knew what was about to unfold.

As I would become aware later during my days at Saint Finbarr's, Father Slattery's antics at getting things done often bordered on craziness. He was a renegade of a person. He had a penchant for the unexpected. His ways of doing things were replete with surprises, wonderment, curiosity, and suspense. He could have been a successful movie star.

He would always find unusual and amusing ways to get things done. That was by a deliberate design by him. Through his unconventional approach, he got a lot of attention. Once he got your attention, he could then impose his will on you. People were amused, rather than offended, by his unusual and eccentric ways. He had a volatile temperament to match his odd ways. No one dared challenge him. Everyone waited patiently for him to announce his grand plan. He hesitated in announcing his plan deliberately to keep the audience in suspense and partly to disarm any rancor from the audience. Father Slattery often operated like a shrewd psychologist. He had all kinds of ingenious means of dealing with people. That was why he was so beloved throughout Nigeria. I do not think he ever lost an argument in his heydays. When discussions did not go his way, he would put on a fake tantrum to still get his way. People usually succumbed to him by simply laughing in amazement at his antics. He was an all-encompassing person; reverend, humorist, runner, boxer, and a sportsman to the core. Except for his clergy robes, his restless ways revealed no sign that he was a Catholic priest. It was not until his later years, in a slowed state of physical being, that anyone could rein him in.

With all the suspense over, Father Slattery announced that the clerks would start reading names off the pile of common entrance examination results. The pile of computer paper contained the list of common entrance results in merit order. Names would be read from the list until the three highest scoring boys in the audience were identified. This process was baffling because there was no way to ensure when the three names would be found among those kids in the audience. Father maintained that if all the kids in the audience had taken the common entrance examination in Lagos, then their names would appear somewhere in the list of results, even if they were at the far end of the list. Father Slattery said he was prepared to continue this exercise until the highest three had been identified, even if it took days. Being enmeshed in the crowd, I heard hisses from some parents. Were they prepared to commit that kind of indefinite time, with no assurance of success in the end? Some parents tried to get Father's attention for private discussions. He refused. Even the highly placed, obviously rich, and well-connected parents in the audience could not sway Father Slattery from his determined approach. Many parents tensely tried to explain the process to their kids. Being alone, I had no one to explain anything to me. Instead, I eavesdropped on the covert mumblings deep within the recesses of the crowd.

Unconcerned, Father Slattery motioned to the clerks to start reading out the names. We embarked on this journey of the endless reading of names. I started praying fervently inwardly to be one of the three selected. Being of small stature, and having only myself to account for, I gradually pushed my way to the front of the crowd. I positioned myself right in front of the clerks' table. I was occasionally pushed back by one of the clerks, wanting to create sufficient elbow room for the prevailing task. At one time, Father Slattery threatened to end the process if the audience crowded the clerks too closely. But realizing the anxiety among the audience, he relented. So, my position was secured close to the face of the person reading the names.

Names were read on and on. The process continued for several hours without anyone acknowledging the names read so far. Being at the edge of the table, I could scan each page of the list as soon as the clerk opened it before the reading of that page started. When my name was not on the list, I would pray silently so that no one else in the audience would be on that page. The process had started around 9a.m. It must have been around 1p.m. when the first name of the audience was found. The first successful name found was Francis Egbuniwe.

One position out of three was gone. I only had two more chances to enter Saint Finbarr's College. I intensified my silent prayers. The second successful name found was Joseph Molokwu.

After what seemed like days, I spotted my name about the middle of a newly opened page. I screamed, "That's my name, that's my name, on this page, that's my name." "My name is here!" sticking my finger at my name listed on the page. This unauthorized announcement caught everyone off guard. I was shouted at to keep quiet. Names must be read from the top to the bottom. There would be no interjection to the middle of the page. When the clerk got to that point, the name would be called. I further intensified my silent prayers. "God, let no one else be called ahead of my name on that page." I am sure that the Good Lord was listening to my juvenile prayers. The third, and final successful name found was Bodunde Badiru.

Although the passage of time has eroded my recollection of the exact events of that day, the agony of the tense waiting has remained etched in my memory. In later years at the school, Francis, Joseph, and I, along with Joseph's close friend, Michael Elumeze, would engage in endless debates as to who was picked first, second, or third. I still feel the torment of waiting to be picked third. I remember the order clearly. Father Slattery came back onto the scene to formalize the selection of the three kids. He announced that these three kids were the new students at Saint Finbarr's College.

1. **Francis Egbuniwe (now late)**
2. **Joseph Molokwu**
3. **Bodunde Badiru**

They must show up to start classes in the morning, without delay. School had already started two weeks earlier. So, we must start attending classes forthwith.

I began my secondary school education at Saint Finbarr's College in January 1968. Father Slattery oversaw the admission process his own way. It was fair, just, and transparent. It was right there in the open field. No flattery, no pretensions. There were no private meetings. There were no under-the-table deals. It was the only way I could have entered a reputable secondary school in 1968. All other doors had been slammed shut. Father Slattery opened the door of educational opportunity for me, without consideration of age, color, creed, race, tribe, language, financial status, political leaning, or religious affiliation. It was totally based on merit. He let the best in the pool of prospective students rise to the top to claim the three prized positions. Can you see my point now? It was a special blessing for me. I hope readers can now understand why writing this book is incredibly special for me. I cannot imagine going to my grave without committing this story to a published book. I am extraordinarily indebted to Father Slattery. Writing this book is the only way I can reward his kindness and fairness. Leaders of today and tomorrow should learn a lot from Father Slattery's ways.

My life has been intimately intertwined with events associated with Saint Finbarr's College. My life then and my life now still bear remarkable allegiance to some memorable events during my days at the school. I had many good times at Saint Finbarr's College. My classmates from those Finbarr's days are still my friends today, to whatever extent we can still stay connected and in touch. The fun of my Class IIIA and the faces in our class photo remain etched in my memory.

Mr. Kpotie, who later became a Finbarr's principal, was our biology teacher in that class year. I often served as the illustrator for biology class. As the teacher wrote notes on the board, I drew biology drawings to accompany the notes. My Biology, Chemistry, and Physics notes were always complete and well-illustrated, and many times, my classmates borrowed my notebooks to make up their own notes at home. Using my artistic interest, I hand-embossed Saint Finbarr's logo on the cover of each notebook.

I enjoyed my biology, chemistry, and physics lessons so much that I later coined the following quote on the subjects, with respect to my 2010 book on **"The Physics of Soccer: Using Math and Science to Improve Your Game."**

> *"Biology determines what we are, Chemistry explains what makes us what we are, and Physics describes what we do."* - Deji Badiru

I was particularly close to all my classmates, but those that I ran around town with most often were Joseph Molokwe, Michael Elumeze, and Abimbola Aibinu. My relationships cut across all genres of classmates. Other close classroom associates were Babatunde Ogunde, Olawale Adewoyin, Philip Bieni, Charles Azoume, and the late Francis Egbuniwe.

My passion for reading and writing extensively originated from my days at Saint Finbarr's College. My series of books on the Physics of Soccer (2010, 2014, and 2018) were inspired by the sports legacy acquired at Saint Finbarr's College. My Finbarr's ID card and my Ebute-Metta neighborhood soccer club ID card are two of my most cherished items from those days. Father Slattery personally signed my Finbarr's ID card himself, as he did for all students at that time.

In my Finbarr's days, I read voraciously by checking out books from the Yaba Public Library. I, especially, loved the American Cowboy Western Novels for their exceptionally expressive description of the rugged terrains and tough cowboys.

I have remained in true and in frequent touch with Saint Finbarr's College. During my induction into the Nigerian Academy of Engineers (NAE) in 2006, a team of SFC students attended and participated in the great accomplishment. I was as proud of the students' SFC vests as they were of my NAE induction regalia. As an ex-Finbarrian, I continue to participate in promoting SFC at home and abroad in consonant with fellow ex-Finbarrians.

Starting at Saint Finbarr's College was not easy at first. Since I had to start classes the very next day after I was miraculously admitted, I was unprepared. I had no uniform, no school shoes, and no books. My sister, the late Mrs. Durosimi (Mrs. Shojobi at that time) had generously agreed to pay my school fees. However, the arrangement was for my mother to pay for my books, uniforms, and other essential items. Therein lay the initial obstacles. My mother was not immediately prepared for such responsibilities. She was a petty trader, plying her migrant trade between Ondo Township, Atijere, Okitipupa, Ejinrin, and Epe. She was so overjoyed that I had gained admission into a secondary school that she pledged to sell her prized jewelry and family heirlooms to raise the money needed to conduct her own end of the bargain. Selling those things required time. There was a time lag between when I had to start classes and when my mother could buy my uniforms, shoes, and books.

Father Slattery allowed me to attend classes for one whole week without uniform before sending me home. This was an unmistakable message that I needed to get my school uniform by hook or crook. Somehow my mother was able to find the money for my uniform. As for the books, Father Slattery allowed me to borrow some books from the school library. Gradually, I settled into the business of my secondary school education.

Although Father Slattery knew me personally at that time because of the way I entered the school, what really brought us close together was a miscue that I committed in his religious studies class. In one of the early examination questions that I faced in his class, I missed the definition of immaculate conception. What I presented as the definition was the exact opposite of the answer. The error must have been due to my lack of knowledge or a temporary gap in my train of thought. I cannot quite explain how the error occurred, but Father Slattery was furious. He said I committed blasphemy. "Son, you have sinned. The thing you should have done was to not write anything if you knew you did not know the answer," he exclaimed. "I will have to pray for you." He made a big deal of the issue not just because of the error itself, but because he wanted to make sure that I got the message. Indeed, I got the message. That incident encouraged me to never let any point of religious studies slide through my fingers again. Thereafter, I became one of the best students in Father

Slattery's classes. This is an example of how Father Slattery used shrewd antics to get the attention of students. It was a clever mind game that he played to get students to perform at their best.

Discipline was and still is a major attribute and attraction of Saint Finbarr's College. Parents take delight in the discipline that kids get at school. The mantra of the school revolves around three tenets of:

1. **Academics**
2. **Football**
3. **Discipline**

The school was widely noted for these. Father Slattery provided the educational infrastructure to pursue academics. He also provided the sports environment to ensure the accomplishment of an esteemed football prowess. Finally, he conjured the physical presence to impose discipline on everyone. There was a rule for everything. Abiding by those rules helped in shaping the outlook of the students.

Cartoon experiments in the art room of Saint Finbarr's led to a brief opportunity to draw cartoon strips for the children's page of the Daily Times of Nigeria newspaper in 1970 and 1971. My cartoon column was dubbed **"Fun with BB."** The art teacher and Father Slattery were proud of this "educational outreach" as they called it because I had a contract and got paid for the cartoons that were published in the newspaper. This was a big accomplishment for a high school kid in those days. Father Slattery was particularly impressed because the school was still relatively young and needed to build a good reputation in other areas apart from football. He would widely commend and publicize any outside accomplishments of students at the school.

The Daily Times of Nigeria Limited

Printers and Publishers of Daily Times, Sunday Times, Sporting Record, Spear Magazine, Woman's World, Home Studies, Lagos Weekend, Insight, Nigeria Year Book and Teacher's Journal

3 Kakawa Street, Lagos
P.O. Box 139
Telephone 25611 (9 lines)
Telegrams TIMES LAGOS
Cables DAILY TIMES LAGOS

28 June, 1972.

Dear Master Badiru,

I received your letter containing the cartoons and I have spoken to both the Editor of the Daily Times and the Editor of the Art Studio, and I have been asked to contact you.

Mr Ayo Ajayi, Editor of Times Art Studio, has shown great interest in your contributions and he has asked me to tell you to send more, as many as possible so that he will be able to plan them to appear weekly in the Children's Times column. This he thinks will surely encourage others to send in their contributions. The Editor of the Daily Times, Mr Odukomaiya, is also wholly for this venture.

The question of the sum to be awarded for the contributions will be decided later and I will surely contact you. In the meantime please send as many as you can. The French ones will also be welcome.

Due to technical reasons some of the cartoons may have to be re-arranged for more effectiveness. We hope this will not be to your disapproval. We hope to hear from you soon.

Yours faithfully,

H.A. Akapo

Ag. Children's Times Editor

Directors: Alhaji Babatunde Jose (Chairman) · Lady Ayodele Alakija · Gordon Philip Cassdy (British) · Labas Ngati Nwanze (Cameroonian)

While I was at Saint Finbarr's, I played on the mosquito and rabbit football teams. These were the junior level teams designed to prepare boys for the full-fledged first-eleven team later. My self-proclaimed nickname for playing football was "Iron Pillar." Some of my fun-loving classmates (notably Benedict Ikwenobe) translated the nickname into different variations. These invoked a lot of fun and laughter whenever we were on a playing field. Although I was a decent player, I was never committed to being on the regular team of Saint Finbarr's College. Late Mr. Anthony

Onoera (former principal), while coaching our rabbit team, lamented that if I would fully commit to playing football, I could be a superb Finbarr's player. Of course, the competition for securing a spot on the regular team was incredibly keen and I was not fully committed to training to be a regular soccer player. Saint Finbarr's College football players were of a different stock – highly skilled and talented. Many of them, even in high school, could have played on professional teams. In fact, the 1970 team was so good that there was a plan to have the team play the professional team Stationery Stores. Te sudden death of Chief Israel Adebajo, the owner of Stationery Stores, one day before the scheduled match, scuttled the plan. We never got to find out if our high school team could have beaten a full-fledged professional team. In my later years, recalling my Saint Finbarr's soccer heritage, I blossomed into a more respectable recreational player. I played on my university team in Tennessee and later adult recreational teams in Florida and Oklahoma.

Inter-house sports were another big part of the experience at Saint Finbarr's College. Although I participated in several sports at the school, I was always only on the fringes of excellence in each one. My primary goal was to be more a part of the fun of sports. I do not recall devoting the necessary training time needed to excel. I occasionally used the pretext of going for sports training at the school to escape from home so that I could go and play elsewhere. My sister always gave me permission to go out if I connected the reason to some sports activity at the school. She knew sports were important at Saint Finbarr's and she never wanted to interfere with the school's expectations.

Following my enrollment at Saint Finbarr's College, I occasionally stayed with my sister at the Unilag Staff Quarters. Whenever she did not have house help, I would move in with her to provide household support covering all manners of household chores including kitchen service and gardening. My present affinity for the kitchen and household chores was shaped in those years. Living so close to the college often created temptations for us to sneak out of school during school hours. This was against the rules of the school, but young boys always enjoy the challenge (and perils) of doing what they are told not to do. If we managed to sneak out without being caught by Father Slattery, we would visit the homes of classmates living at Akoka and make the long trek to Lagoon at the edge of Unilag campus – in search of fun. Thinking back now, it was a significant risk. I can never explain why we would have risked being expelled from the school. Whenever we successfully snuck out and arrived at the school compound, we were filled with a sense of great accomplishment. With that euphoria, we started looking forward to the next opportunity to sneak out again. I thank God that no one in my group of friends was ever caught engaging in this mischievous act. Boys that were caught faced the full wrath of Father Slattery. I did my best to stay out of such wrath. In fact, I earned a good Testimonial from Father Slattery when I graduated. He was never bashful to write straight testimonials, whether good or bad. He signed every document directly by himself. Original documents signed by Father Slattery are highly priced documents by those who had the good fortune to have received a signed document from him.

A December 1998 Christmas Card from Father Slattery to the Badiru Family contains his usual statements of blessings. The card remains a cherished item in the family's collection of memorable items. The greetings, in Father Slattery's own aged handwriting, reads as follows:

"Dear Adedeji B. Badiru

Congratulations for all the letters from U.S. and thank you for the Video. Received it here in Ireland on Twenty-third November 1998.

I hope a member of my family will tape it and send a copy to our Boss – Blackrock Road, Cork. It will be kept in the Archives and probably used occasionally to help the cause of the Mission.

I was very proud of all the old boys who appeared on the Video. Your speeches were wonderful. You made it a historic and unique occasion.

You will be happy to know that I am all set for my return journey to Lagos –

I hope to continue for some time the work of the Mission and pay a special attention to Finbarr's and the old boys and the new.

Thanks for all you have done for the Alma Mater.

Greet your wife and children. May God Bless you all.

Happy and holy Christmas.

God bless you.

Denis Slattery"

It is a fact that Saint Finbarr's College adequately prepared me for the challenges, tribulations, and triumphs of life following my completion of my secondary school education. This is the same story that every graduate of the school proudly proclaims. Around town, Finbarr's boys enjoyed special privileges, which many were quick to flaunt. "Omo Father Slattery" (Father Slattery's kid) was a common moniker for Finbarr's boys around Lagos in those days.

By the time I graduated from Saint Finbarr's College in December 1972, my days of reckless fun were ending. 1970 represented the height of my enjoyment of Lagos streets. Starting in 1973, several other things were beginning to creep into my life. I still wanted to continue my association with my neighborhood friends. I belonged to informal clubs dedicated to having fun in the neighborhoods. There was the Lagos Island Rascals and The Kano Street Gang at Ebute Metta. In 1966, I lived with my uncle at Bamgbose Street right across from Campus Square. I made several friends on the tough playgrounds of campus square. In my various living arrangements with relatives between 1961 and 1972, I had resided at various locations in the Lagos Metropolis. I had lived at Andrew Street, Lagos; Tokunboh Street, Lagos; Bamgbose Street, Lagos; Ita Alagba Street, Lagos; Kano Street, Ebute Metta; Brickfield Road, Ebute Metta; Bode Thomas Street, Surulere; and University of Lagos Staff Quarters.

Even after finishing secondary school, I still enjoyed cruising many of the fun neighborhoods of my previous habitats. My family started to worry about my future. They were concerned that I was too nonchalant and indifferent about my future. They deplored my interest in attending parties in Lagos. They wanted me to aggressively start seeking admission to a university. But I would always defend myself by claiming that I knew "what I was doing." I maintained that I had everything under control. Underneath the party image, I had a structured and determined mind focused on being successful with whatever I wanted to do. Father Slattery had impacted the discipline of success on all his students; and I was sure I was not going to end up destitute. My attitude was "Let me enjoy myself for now; success is destined to come later on."

The fact that I met and married my wife was a coincidence that had its roots in the Art Room of Saint Finbarr's College. If I had not attended Saint Finbarr's College and returned to the painting of the colorful rooster, I would not be married to my wife today. It was a stepwise progression from Saint Finbarr's College art room to the eventual liaison with my future wife.

I was a good student of Art, and our art teacher took a special interest in my future professional outlook. He felt that I was good enough to become a renowned professional artist. Being somewhat of an all-rounder, each of my other teachers had expressed similar expectations that I would go into a profession fitting his or her own subject. The French teacher, Mr. Akinrimade, expected me to become a professional in the Nigerian foreign mission with assignments to French-speaking countries. He later tried to get me to attend the Nigerian Defense Academy (NDA), thinking that I would make a great Army officer in Nigeria's missions in the African Francophone countries. The biology teacher, Mr. A. A. Kpotie, who later became principal, advised that I should go into the medical field. The English teacher hoped that I followed his profession and become an English teacher, writer, or poet. The Physics teacher suggested that I would make an excellent scientist. My Mathematics teacher wanted me to become an engineer. Observing my later performance in his own Religious Studies class, Father himself thought I would be a good religious ambassador, bridging the division between Christians and Moslems. As for me, I just went with the flow. I did not pay much attention to what the future held for me in terms of a profession. I believed in existentialism and adapted to whatever came up for the moment. Enjoying the moment was all that mattered to me.

CHAPTER 4

GREAT TIMES AT FINBARR'S: NEXUS OF SOCCER AND ACADEMICS

Many superior soccer players have walked the halls of Saint Finbarr's College over the years. I particularly remember the golden years of Finbarr's soccer when I attended the school from 1968 to 1972. I remember the epic championship games of the secondary school principal's cup of Lagos in that era. Notable names like John Emilio and Ibeh. I remember the wild celebrations following the classic wins. Sadly, I also remember the celebratory accident on the school's lorry that took the life of one my classmates and close friend, Ekong Udoffia. He had climbed on top of the roof of the school lorry after an epic soccer glory at Onikan Stadium in the heart of Lagos. He fell off the roof in the congested traffic and died. My school lecture notes were with him during the weekend that he died. I am eternally grateful to his family for dutifully returning the notes to me within a few days to ensure that I did not suffer any academic impediment because of the disastrous loss. I still have those notes (Biology, Physics, and Chemistry) today and I often proudly display them to my children and colleagues as a testament to the academic legacy of Saint Finbarr's College. Photos of the covers of the notes are shown in Chapter One of this book.

There are many exceptional stories of the great times at Saint Finbarr's College, where academics, discipline, and soccer are intertwined. Most stories center around academics and soccer.

Some of the stories are old news, but reinforcement and repetition are a good thing for promoting the prestige and legacy of Saint Finbarr's College. The testimony below was written in 2020 to commemorate the 64th anniversary of the school. Thus, references are for 2022. It is noted that the 66th anniversary happened on September 25th, 2022.

September 25th, 2020 was the 64th Anniversary of our great Alma Mater Saint Finbarr's College. It is the feast of our patron St. Finbarr's of Cork founded on January 10th, 1956, exactly sixty-four years ago by our indefectible principal very Revd. Fr. Denis Joseph Slattery SMA aka "Oga" as one of the founding pupils, I recollect vividly the poor start of St. Finbarr College from the embryonic stage. The school started with three (3) borrowed classroom from St. Paul Catholic Primary School Apapa Road, Ebute Metta. The Manager of St. Paul's Catholic School Revd. Fr. McCarthy agreed to borrow Fr. Slattery the founded and principal of St. Finbarr College these three classrooms to start St. Finbarr's College. There were sixty-four founding pupils in two (2) classes Forms 1A & 1B while the third room served as the principal's office, the teaching staff room with only two pioneer staff Messers A. O. Bankole and Ferdinand Ejieke and the Secretary/bursars office. This multipurpose room served as a First Aid depot and the library, in essence every information about the school is from this office Thus, if the principal sneezed in his office all the pupils and the members of staff would feel it were ever, they were. There were borrowed benches and tables together with one blackboard for two classes and rags for cleaning. Nine subjects were ably managed by the 3 pioneer teachers including the principal himself. The principal took charge of Religious Knowledge, English Language and Latin. Mr. Bankole took charge of Arithmetic, Algebra, Geometry (they were separate subjects in those days) and General Science while Mr. Ejieke was incharge of History and Geography. Playing Football started on the very day we resumed on the borrowed pitch of St. Paul's School. Our first match was played against our host St. Paul's on the June 29th,1956 (feast of Ss. Peters and Paul). He lost 0-2. The first feast of our Alma Mater was a free day for us on the September 25th, 1956 (Feast of St. Finbarr's of Cork). *Missa Cantata* (Sung Mass) was celebrated in one of the classrooms by the principal while the sermon was delivered by Revd. Fr. Dr. Joseph Adeneye, the Principal of St. Joseph Teachers Training College Surulere. The Mass Serves were Dunstan Openibo and Patrick Koshoni (Jnr.) as MCs, Frederick Ogundipe (myself) and Benard Koshoni (Snr.) were the two acolytes while Paul Okomah conducted the choirs. After that, there was a group photograph of the foundation staff and students on the open field. We had plenty to eat and drink before the inter-house sport to round up the first Anniversary. As one of the pioneer students of St. Finbarrs College from Ebute Metta 1956-1958 and Akoka 1959-1961, I congratulate all Finbarrians in Diaspora on this day. For those that are not alive, I pray to God to rest their souls (RIP). I tried to remember the names of some of my colleagues who started with me in 1956. Not in any order. 1. Patrick Koshoni who designed the logo on the badge that we are using today, teo. Sylvester Ogundana Form 1A Prefect, 3. Sylvester Ogunamana Form 1B Prefect, 4. Godffrey Bechi, 5. Paul James, 6. Robert Adedipe, 7. Gerald Adekoya, 8. Sunday Ibezim, 9. Temi Uwejoma, 10. Patrick Adumekwe, 11. Augustine Cocker, 12. Henry Jamougha, 13. Bonaventure Tevi, 14. Julius Anighoro, 15. Christopher Oyemen, 16.

Lawrence Ronald, 17. Oluyole Sojinu, 18. Dunstan Openubo, 19. Benard Koshonu, 20. Francis Wilsin, 21. A. Ayeni, 22. Samson Okon, 23. Felix Oriakhi, 24. Patrick Ezeah, 25. Festus Olafimihan, 26. Michael Okobi, 27. Christopher Madufor, 28. Pius Ojuriye, 29. Fredrick Rickettes, 30. Felix Kotogbe, 31.

Anthony Okudaye, 32. Joseph Oyemena, 33. Felichiano Adeniyi, 34. Paul Okonmah, 35. Fredrick Ogundipe, 36. Alex Tolefe, 37. Albert Jemade, 38.

Francis Adegburin, 39. Joseph Babatunde, 40. Festus Ofilin, 41. David Johnson, 42. Solomon Salako, 43. Mathias Ozogolu, 44. Felechiano Adeniyi, 45. Anthony Beckley, 46. Godwin Ugba, 47. Albert Bankola, 48. Tom Gbora, 49. Joshson Koffi, 50. Stephen Emeana, 51. George Nwagwu, 52. Nwaja, 53. Augustine Fashola, 54. David Green, 55. Dominic Ojelabi, 56. Olaniyi Green, 57. Paul Okapu, 58. Paul Onipede, 59. Sylvester Ogundana, 60. Raymond Alade, 61.

Godfrey Omoshikeji, 62. Stephen Igbonoba, 63. Anthony Nwachukwu, 64.

JamesIgbuwe, 65. Chike Igbonoba, 66. Mike Nwamara, 67. Joseph Martins.

FOUNDATION STAFF AND PUPILS OF ST. FINBARRS COLLEGE, EBUTE METTA LAGOS (25TH SEPTEMBER 1956)

Saint Finbarr's College is solidly represented among the Greatest Soccer Players in the history of the Principal's Cup in Lagos, Nigeria. Some of the notable names are recalled below:

1. Haruna Ilerika - Zumratul Uslamiya Grammar School.
2. Henry Nwosu - Saint Finbarrs College.
3. Tunde Martins - Igbobi College.
4. David Adidi - Saint Gregory.
5. Albert Adidi - ""
6. Ahmed Tandor - Saint Gregory.
7. Eyo Sanaya - Saint Finbarrs College.
8. Chris Oyobio - Saint Finbarrs College.
9. Marcellus Obinatu - Saint Finbarrs College.
10. Cajetan Obinatu - Saint Finbarrs College.

12. Godwin Odiye - Saint Finbarrs College.

13. Bernard Senaya - Saint Finbarrs College.

14. Emilio Adeniyu - Saint Finbarrs College.

15. Ricky Manuela - Saint Finbarrs College.

16. Taju Disu - Ansar Uddeen.

17. K C. Adeniyi - Saint Finbarrs College.

18. Adokiye Amesiemeka - CMS Grammar School.

19. Murtala Onibanjo (Scoro) - Saint Finbarrs College.

20. Goddy Okoroba Okon - CMS.

21. Tony Eyo - Saint Finbarrs College.

22. John Amayo - Saint Finbarrs College.

23. Nathaniel Ogedegbe - Saint Finbarrs College.

24. Emeka James - Saint Finbarrs College.

25. Jaokin Aromu Onela - Saint Finbarrs College.

26. Franklin Howard (Kwani) - Baptist Academy.

27. Nkem Oliseh - Baptist Academy.

28. Emeka Adigwe - Baptist Academy.

29. Sunny Oyobio - MBHS.

30. Eddie Polo (Beach Freeman) - MBHS.

31. Segun Adeleke (Gaskiya) - MBHS.

32. Emmanuel Sonya - MBHS.

33. Maryland Obasanjo - MBHS.

34. Paul Okoku - Saint Finbarrs College.

35. Stephen Keshi - Saint Finbarrs College.

36. Chris Anigala - Saint Finbarrs College.

37. Samson Siasia - Saint Finbarrs College.

38. Wilson Itive - Saint Finbarrs College.

39. Bode Lawal - Baptist Academy.

40. Opeyimi - CMS.

41. Sam Bazuaye (Bazuu) - CMS.

42. Niyi Adadoyin (Palongo) - CMS.

43. Samuel John - CMS Grammar School.

44. Ajagun - Zumratul Islamiya School.

45. Emilo John- St Finbarr's College.

46. Sunny Izevbije - St Finbarr's College.

47. Murtala Onigbanjo (Skoro) - CMS Grammar School.

48. Dayo Martins - Gbobi College.

49. Maxwell Akpan - CMS Grammar School / St Finbarr's College.

50. Adedeji Obe- St Finbarr's College.

51. Victor Opene St Finbarr's College.

52. Okoh- St Finbarr's College.

53. Duru- St Finbarr's College / Baptist Academy.

54. Emmanuel Yola St Finbarr's College / St Gregory's College

55. Jonah Onyo St Finbarr's College.

56. Edemson - St Finbarr's College.

57. Kola Balogun - St Finbarr's College.

58. Anthony Orji - St Finbarr's College.

59. Jackson - St Finbarr's College.

60. Christopher Nwosu (German War) - St Gregory's College.

61. Segun Olukanni - CMS Grammar School.

62. Femi Olukanni - CMS Grammar School.

63. Patrick Obitor - St Finbarr's College.

64. Sam Owoh - St Finbarr's College.

65. Muda Okuribido.

This is an extensive list of Finbarr's Soccer Greats. Unfortunately, it is not possible to include testimonies and profiles of all the greats. Only a select few are included in this book due to several factors, including limited page count for the book, Lack of information, inability to locate many individuals, and timing issues.

In the 1969-71 timeframe, one soccer player, Desmond Cardoso, used to go around the school compound with the popular salutation of

"Kadoso-Karamba" to the delight of all students. Those were fun times at Finbarr's.

Past Winner of the Principal's Cup, Lagos, Nigeria

1948: Methodist Boys High School, Lagos

1949: Saint Gregory's College, Obalende

1950: Saint Gregory's College, Obalende

1951: Saint Gregory's College, Obalende

1952: Saint Gregory's College, Obalende

1953: King's College, Lagos

1954: Saint Gregory's College, Obalende

1955: Baptist Academy, Lagos

1956: Saint Gregory's College, Obalende

1957: Ahmadiyya College, Agege

1958: King's College, Lagos

1959: King's College, Lagos

1960: Ahmadiyya College, Agege

1961: Methodist Boys High School, Lagos

1962: Saint Finbarr's College, Akoka

1963: CMS Grammar School, Bariga

1964: Kings College, Lagos

1965: Ahmadiyya College, Agege

1966: Saint Finbarr's College, Akoka

1967: Ahmadiyya College, Agege

1968: Saint Finbarr's College, Akoka

1969: Saint Finbarr's College, Akoka

1970: Zumratul-Islamiya Grammar School, Yaba

1971: Saint Finbarr's College, Akoka

1972: Saint Finbarr's College, Akoka

1973: Saint Finbarr's College, Akoka

1974: No Competition

1975: CMS Grammar School, Bariga

1976: CMS Grammar School, Bariga (defeated Saint Finbarr's)

1977: Saint Finbarr's College, Akoka

1978: Saint Gregory's College, Obalende

1979: Saint Gregory's College, Obalende

1980: CMS Grammar School, Bariga

1981: Saint Gregory's College, Obalende

1982: Saint Gregory's College, Obalende

1983: ???

1984: ???

1985: ???

1986: ???

1987 **Saint Finbarr's College, Akoka** (Defeated Saint Gregory's College)

It is observed that Saint Finbarr's College quickly ascended the level of soccer championship ranks soon after its founding in 1956. The first Finbarr's championship happened in 1962, just six years after emerging on the scene. Except for a couple of interruptions, Finbarr's had a strangle hold on the championship for eight straight years and quickly became a household name among the elite schools of Lagos.

The principal's cup soccer competition was suspended after the 1987 championship due to emerging violence associated with the competition. Finding a sponsor became problematic. The cup's profile has become inconsistent for several reasons. At some point it was sponsored by Malta Guinness company and renamed Malta Guinness Lagos Principals Cup. In more recent times (circa 2010), GTBank became the sponsor. Tracking the competition and recording the winners became more ad hoc.

Further, the competition has been split into two - the Principal's Cup for regular schools (newer and Lagos State Government owned schools) and the Heritage Cup for the older schools (the legacy schools), including Saint

Finbarr's College, Saint Gregory's College, King's College, Methodist Boys High School, Baptist Academy, Ansar-Ud-Deen, and Igbobi College. A female competition has also been created. Hopefully, the glory days of the Principal's Cup can be revived at some point.

Studying the chronology of the events, I cannot deny linking the departure of Father Slattery to the first stage of failure of the glory days of Soccer's Principal's Cup in Lagos. There was a noticeable decline in soccer affairs of secondary schools in Lagos with the absence of the usual flare of Father Slattery.

Father Slattery oversaw Saint Finbarr's College from 1956 until 1976, when it was taken over by the Lagos State Government. Every academic infrastructure, structure of discipline, and sports commitment built by Father Slattery went into a tailspin. Father Slattery was devastated to see his lifelong investment in Saint Finbarr's College go down the political drain of the government.

In 1979, the government introduced free education at all levels, with a mandated taking over of private schools, including Saint Finbarr's College. The free education program, without a solid educational strategy, resulted in an astronomical increase in secondary school enrollment and the consequence was over-crowding and decline in academic excellence.

On the **October 2nd, 2001,** the government approved the return of schools to their initial owners. By the time Saint Finbarr's College was returned to the Church, it had been academically decimated. Over the past 22 years, the school has rebounded with the collective efforts of the Church, the school administration, and the worldwide Old Boys Association. The future of Academics, Discipline, and Soccer is, once again, bright at Saint Finbarr's College.

CHAPTER 5

PAUL OKOKU:
FINBARR'S SOCCER GREAT

St Finbarr's was specifically chosen to be the flag carrier for Nigeria during the open ceremony of the 1980 AFCON tournament. Indeed, it was a proud moment for St. Finbarr's which was chosen for its prestige, leadership in academics, discipline, and success in sports. I was the very person who carried the "placard of Nigeria" during the opening ceremony. It was said that Finbarr's brought good luck to the Green Eagles after winning the first ever AFCON tournament in Nigeria's history.

Paul Okoku at the first reunion of St. Finbarr's College Old Boys' Association (SFCOBA), in Atlanta, 2012.

As one of the players on Coach Adegboyega Onigbinde's Super Eagles Los Angeles, USA, Olympics 1984 (qualifying) team, on October 30, 1983, we defeated the Black Stars, 2 - 1, in the return match in Accra, Ghana, when Chibuzor Ehilegbu and John Omughele scored a goal each. We lost to Morocco in the finals in Rabat, thus Morocco went ahead to represent Africa in the Olympics '84. In the match against Ghana, we'd played a goalless draw two weeks earlier (October 15, 1983) in Kaduna, but—in my humble opinion—Ghana is unarguably Nigeria's most dreaded opponent in football and will always be, bar-none. That much is evident if you grew up in my generation. Football historians will agree. Forget that the 1984 AFCON Super Eagles team started the rivalry between Nigeria and Cameroon when we lost to them in the finals of the AFCON '84. I was a member of that team as well, so I speak from personal experience when I say it didn't compare to our long-standing rivalry with Ghana.

I was a member of the St. Finbarr's College football team in 1981 when we were almost walked over for being over 30 minutes late during the quarter finals of the 1981 principal's cup against the Baptist Academy Secondary School. However, Festus Okunbule, one of the top referees in Nigeria, wasn't going to have it. He gave us the 30 + extra time despite the norm being a 15-minute grace period.

The agony of stress on the faces of students who were crying, and wailing was too much to bear. Even non-students' supporters also cried. Nonetheless, we went on to defeat Baptist Academy High School football team 3 goals to nil.

I was invited to join over 200 other non-students football players for screening on a Saturday morning and the multitude of players who showed up underscored the dignity and reputation Finbarr's commanded as a breeding ground for talents discovery.

I was unfortunately exposed to the infamous "station one" where students who skipped classes / school would converge. My first day there was also my last, because the Principal, Mr. Aloysius Kpotie, came to raid the spot.

Right after one of our practices, the principal called for a meeting for the players in front of his office. It was then that he announced that I was going to be the school captain for the 1981 set. That didn't go well as I respectfully declined the offer mainly because there were two players who had been on the team a year or two before me—one of whom was eventually made the captain. He went on a pressured campaign and negative crusade turning people against me, Mr. Kpotie who was the principal and coach Malagu. I was made one of the two vice captains. However, the threat of voodoo became glaringly apparent as this individual told us that he will travel to his West African country to get the voodoo he would cast on us. Due to that revelation, my roommate and I began going to school and practice from our respective homes rather than staying on the school's boys' quarter. Despite my respectful decline of the lodging offer, the controversy became a distraction. As a result, I was held accountable for losing to CMS Grammar School in the semifinals in 1981 for declining to be the team's captain. Evidently, the Coach told me that we did not advance to the finals because of my humble decision as it was revealed to them in prayer that if I became the captain, we would have won the principal's cup for that year, 1981. Nonetheless, CMS eventually won the 1981 Principal Cup.

The Principal, Mr. Kpotie, and the late Coach Malagu reminded me of the incident during our presentation of educational technology (learning) equipment to St. Paul's Primary School, Ebute Metta, West. This was in 2014, courtesy of myself, the late Stephen Keshi and Godwin odiye. Additionally, during Mr. Kpotie's speech at the event, he reminded us of St. Finbarr's started from St. Paul's Catholic Primary School, Apapa Rd, Ebute Metta, West, before relocating to Akoka.

A popular belief in circulation at the time claimed that Finbarr's players were non-students and usually were not academically inclined. I beg to differ and would like to highlight the academic success of some of the players. The following Finbarr's players who also were in the Nigerian National teams, Flying Eagles and Super Eagles, were college graduates. They include Godwin Odiye, Bernard Senaya, Chris Oyobio, Martin Eyo, Emilo John, Emeka James, Christopher Anigala, Dennis Echefu, Nathaniel Ogedegbe and Obe Adedeji just to name a few.

Mrs. Duncan secretly called me away from the administrative office to outside of the building after Principal Kpotie had introduced me to the teaching staff as a former footballer and a student who passed his WAEC at the first attempt. She did all that to find out if I took and passed her subject, Literature, during WAEC. I told her affirmatively, yes. She then took me back into the office to reintroduce me as one of her students, and a football player, who took and passed Literature. That was hilarious!

Mr. Kpotie kept me in suspense on the day I went for my WAEC results in a long line of both happy and unhappy students after getting their WAEC results. When it was my turn, I went into his office and he instructed me to "sit down, Paul. Wait for me until I am done giving results to the students", he's said.

I sat there as it was torturing asking myself why I was singled out. I sat down gracing the precious (football-like trophy) gift I had bought him from Sweden a year before still looking brand new.

We were waking up at 5am for football practices and jogging to and from the University of Lagos field in time to make it to class after a scrimmage. We would bathe and wind up with no time for food, but we still prioritized getting to class. Those were the sacrifices we made to bring glory to the school and maintain our respect as a footballing institution. It was an indisputable culture.

Other times, when it was lunch period, we knew what was on the menu. Yes, that ever-popular, high-and-mighty meat pie; we would do justice to it.

Attending St. Finbarr's exposed me to some children whose parents were wealthy and famous. Children of the "Who's Who" in the community. For instance, I was in the same class with Lanre, the son of the late former Governor of Lagos State, Brigadier Mobolaji Johnson.

I can remember a dark day of my St. Finbarr's off campus experience. I almost witnessed one of our 1981 team members get lynched. He was erroneously singled out as a thief after we had just had a meal at station 2. As the crowd grew larger, they became overpowering, shouting out "Ole, ole!" Others were attempting to place a tire around his neck and set him ablaze, an infamous punishment for thieves at the time. Thank God that there were people who recognized us as Finbarr's football players and came to his rescue. That was a scary moment.

The same Mrs. Duncan had asked us to stand on our respective desks and made inquiries for each of our names. Incidentally, we all had English names. She then instructed us to go back home and to tell our parents to change our English names to native names because of not being able to recite a poem from memory in front of our classmates. Funny enough, today, over 40 years after graduating from St. Finbarr's I can still recite that very poem in my sleep because she drilled it into our skull: "Out, out, brief candle! Life's but a walking shadow, a poor player that struts and frets his hour upon the stage and then is heard no more: it is a tale told by an idiot, full of sound and fury, signifying nothing." --**Macbeth from "The Tragedy of Macbeth" (Act V, Scene V)**.

Playing in the 1984 AFCON finals in Ivory Coast with two other Finbarrians, late Stephen Keshi (captain) and Henry Nwosu, was a proud moment for me. The AFCON is the highest football tournament in Africa.

We won the silver medals and made history for being the first Super Eagles team to advance to the finals of an AFCON hosted outside Nigeria since the inception of the tournament. Nigeria won it as the host in 1980 (in Nigeria). We managed to do what no Super Eagles team before us could under the leadership of an indigenous manager, Coach Adegboyega Onigbinde.

Another moment of proud and pride for me as a Finbarrian occurred when I was named the Vice Captain of the first ever Nigerian team to play in any FIFA organized tournament (U21). The U21 World Cup tournament took place in Mexico, 1983. We played against the likes of Marco Van Basten—the three-time European best player—Bebeto, Geovani Silva and Dunga (who later captained Brazil's Senior World Cup winning team and coached the Brazilian World Cup winning team in South Africa). The late Ernest Okonkwo nicknamed me "Midfield Dynamo," during our match, Super Eagles, against Morocco in Rabat, on Sunday, the 28th of August 1983, to qualify for the 1984 AFCON.

As a sojourner, Father Slattery changed my life and the lives of so many others by allowing us to attend such a reputable institution of athletic and academic excellence.

As a Founder and CEO of a non-profit organization called Greater tomorrow Children's Fund. We have changed and continue to change and impact the lives of so many underprivileged children in the United States of America and Nigeria.

As one of the founders of the SFCOBA, during our first ever meeting, I met Dr. Badiru for the first time at Kenny Kuku's residence along with Dr. Samuel Duru. We were treated to Nigerian delicious cuisines by Mrs. Mercy Kuku.

During the 1980 AFCON tournament, Mr. Kpotie, and coach Malagu would travel to the Super Eagles camp to pray with and for the Finbarrians on the team: Godwin Odiye, Henry Nwosu and Martin Eyo. It was a deserving honor for the St. Finbarr's community to have three Finbarrians on that AFCON winning team.

Before attending St. Finbarr's College as an observant from the outside, I always thought that St. Gregory's College was a sister school to St. Finbarr's. With that thought in mind, I did not understand why we had to visit CMS at their school camp to pledge our support for them against St. Gregory's after they defeated us in the semifinals; we prayed with them and encouraged them to defeat St. Gregory's in the finals.

We had a prayer meeting with the founding father of Saint Finbarr's College, Father Slattery at his church before our semifinals match against CMS in 1980, Stephen Keshi was the team's captain. All Finbarr's current and former students, their parents, and the worshippers prayed for us. They also donated money on our behalf and sang special hymns for the occasion.

Life at the boys' quarters was fulfilling. We had fun, and we made our education a top priority. It afforded us the best available time for studies because after each practice we would rest in our respective rooms to have energy afterwards to complete homework assignments and have more organized and regulated times for additional studies. We also took the opportunity to receive help in mathematics and science from the academically gifted students.

Oga, aka Principal Kpotie was more than a father figure to us; he was a role model which he gladly took on. It wasn't intentional at first, but it happened naturally through supporting the sports programs over the years.

Stephen Keshi and I met in our preteen years at St. Paul's Primary School. While I attended St. Paul's, he attended Ebenezer Primary School. We played against each other and eventually became childhood companions borne out of our on-the-field rivalry. Before attending Finbarr's, Keshi and I used to attend the senior lits at Saint Finbarr's. We'd had our admiration for the instruction as Catholic students, but our adoration only increased as we witnessed their glorious football successes and their simple ways of achieving said success. Their customs included kneeling down on the field after scoring goals, the story of the founder, Father Slattery.

Before and during our preparations for our WAEC, Segun Olukanni, who was at the time a graduate of Lagos City College and was enrolled in the HSC program at CMS Grammar School, would meet us; myself, Dennis Echefu, Sunday Joseph and Christopher Anigala at our St. Finbarr's boys' quarters at night. We would proceed to the University of Lagos (Unilag) campus and then to Yaba College of Technology for studies and if NEPA took power (light) we had our candles readily available. At Yaba Tech., we suffered harassment from student members of the man-o-war organization. They forcefully pursued us, trashed our books and commanded us to leave. Nonetheless, we weren't deterred because our determined attitude towards our education was not to be pushed aside.

When I went for my WAEC results, Oga told me that "with these results, you can attend any higher institution in Nigeria." That was an amazing feeling in that moment in time for me to receive such commendation from Mr. Kpotie for my academic achievements.

I, Emmanuel Akpan, Femi Olukanni and Bala Ali did get admission into the University Ibadan. Despite this, University of Ile Ife came calling for me as well immediately after playing for the Super Eagles in a friendly match against them on their field. And that match, in 1984, was Rasheed Yekini's first ever game for Nigeria.

Football was almost comparable to a religion at St. Finbarr's--its importance right behind our catholic faith.

St. Finbarr's started at St. Paul's Primary School, at Apapa Road & Costain bus stop. This was before they moved to Akoka. Its academic attainment cannot be overemphasized as many graduates of the institution have gone to and received highest level of education as well as professional successes in Nigeria and across the globe.

Equally, the athletic achievements by the school are no coincidence as it was designed to be this way by the founder, the late Father Slattery. He was personally and intentionally charged with making St. Finbarr's gain notoriety in sports, so he went on to recruit famous students from other schools and groomed his in-house students to stardom. St. Finbarr's became one of the most dreaded high schools of our generation in football.

St. Finbarr's had the highest number student-athletes who played for the Super Eagles which was called Green Eagles then. Nonetheless, from the dialogue I had with Segun Odegbami, MON, he thinks that St. Finbarr's comes second to his high school St. Murumba, Jos. which, in my opinion, is highly arguable and debatable. Clearly and unarguably, St. Finbarr's had the highest number of players who played for the Super Eagles bar-none.

The Youth Sports Federation of Nigeria (YSFON) team, 1980, 1981 & 1982 sets, who won the Gothia Cup in Sweden and won the Dallas Cup in the USA, had five Finbarrians on the team, namely: Paul Okoku, Deputy Captain, Samson Siasia, Raymond King, Christopher Anigala and Alphonsus Akhahon. The players were also members of the Flying Eagles 1983 set to the U21 World Cup in Mexico, 1983.

In 1980, Super Eagles of Nigeria won their first ever AFCON tournament for Nigeria had three students from St. Finbarr's College: Godwin Odiye, Henry Nwosu and Martin Eyo.

For the first time in the history of Nigeria, the Super Eagles reached the finals of the 1984 AFCON outside Nigeria and won the silver medal. Albeit the team lost to Cameroon in the finals, who paraded top African footballers in Roger Milla, Theophilo Abega, Kunde Emmanuel and Thomas Nkono, to mention a few. That 1984 AFCON silver winning Super Eagles team had three players from St. Finbarr's college: Stephen Keshi, Captain, Paul Okoku and Henry Nwosu.

In 1983, Nigeria's Flying Eagles, the under 21 (U21) team, was the first team in the history of Nigeria to qualify Nigeria to any FIFA-organized tournament. This tournament was for the U21 World Cup held in Mexico in 1983. There were five players from St. Finbarr's College: Paul Okoku (who was the deputy captain), Samson Siasia, Raymond King, Christopher Anigala and Alphonsus Akhahon. The team was awarded full scholarships to university level at any University of their choice in the world.

The team played against some of the best players in Africa and in the world, the likes of Youssouf Fofana, Oumar Ben Salah of Ivory Coast, Ndlovu brothers of Zimbabwe. They also played against the likes of, Geovani Siva, Bebeto, Jorginho and Dunga all of Brazil, and several players from Holland including: Erik Boogaard, Sonny Silooy, John Van't Schip, Gerald Vanenburg, and Marco **Van Basten** who was named the FIFA **World Player of** the **Year** in 1992 and won the Ballon d'Or three times, in 1988, 1989 and 1992. He was named "**UEFA best Player of the Year**" three times (1989, 1990 and 1992).

Today, December 29, 2022, my childhood hero, Pele, aka Edson Arantes do Nascimento, of Brazil, a three-time world cup winner, passed away. I had the chance to meet him in 1976 when he was invited to Nigeria under the sponsorship of Pepsi as a brand ambassador for the company for a coaching clinic for youth development at the Liberty stadium, Ibadan. I was a member of the team and one of the participants in the training camp and so was the late Stephen Keshi, a Finbarrian, who was also a member of the team and our team captain. Other three Finbarrians, Raymond King, Dennis Echefu and Sunday Joseph were on the team as well. The team was called Greater Tomorrow under the guidance and sponsorship of the Nigerian Football Association (NFA). A Yugoslavian, named Coach Rocky, was our coach who also led us to Ibadan to meet Pele. As a world cup player himself, coach Rocky played against Pele. He was formerly the assistant coach to Father Tiko, who was the Green Eagles Coach before he was assigned to Greater Tomorrow. Rest In Peace Pele!!!

Yet, another great Conqueror, Bernard Senaya, died on the 5th of December 2022. I was happy that he joined us for our reunion to celebrate our alma mater, St. Finbarr's College Old Boys Association (SFCOBA), in Dayton, Ohio, on the 17th of August 2019. He was sensational on the field of play and exemplified professionalism to the core. Rest In Peace Bernard.

"Education is not a guarantee for success, but without it you don't stand a chance."

By Paul Okoku
Flying Eagles (VC)
Super Eagles Legend

The quote in this display confirms the "academics first" legacy of Saint Finbarr's College.

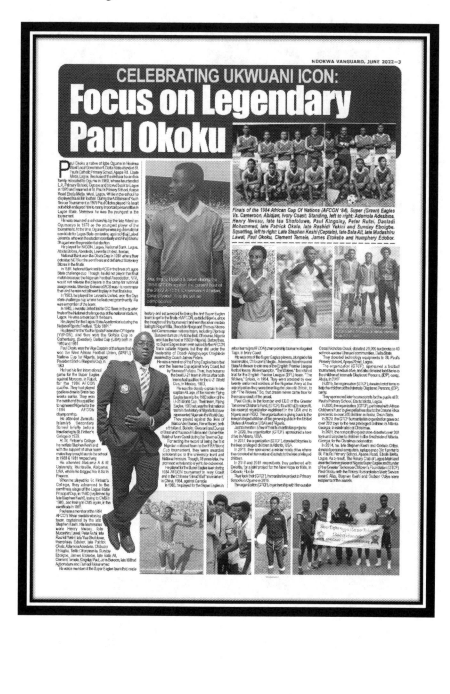

111

In the Photo: Vincent Onyeama, Joseph Yobo (captain), late Stephen Keshi (chief Coach), Paul Okoku (Founder & CEO) and Mikel Obi!

This picture was taken during the Super Eagles pre-2014 World Cup friendly match against the United States Men's National Soccer Team, in Jacksonville, Florida, June 2013. Following Father Slattery's legacy and his contributions to humanity and humanitarian efforts and his mandate to us to charitable (assisting those in need) and to be our brother's keepers. The foundation that was started by a Finbarrian, Paul Okoku, has partnerships with global and reputable organizations. Okoku is also a giver as Founder and CEO, Greater Tomorrow Children's Fund. He provided the following statements:

"Well, by the Special grace of God, we are touching the lives of under privileged children, in the USA and in Nigeria / Africa. A few years ago, we donated 20,000 textbooks to forty schools in Ndokwa, Delta State in collaboration with Hon. Ossai of the Nigerian National House of Assembly.

"We sponsored a football tournament in conjunction with a medical drive for the IDP children in Abuja, Jos, and other areas. We are humbled to be partners with giant companies in the US such as Amazon, Walmart (Good 360), Google (Network for Good), Toys R US and TechSoup.

"Our most recent event took place in December 2021 in the Southside of Atlanta, Georgia where we gave out over two hundred toys and bicycles to children, in time for the Christmas celebration."

Raymond King and Paul Okoku, after St. Finbarr's College defeated **Anwar Islam Ahmadiyah** Grammar School, 1981. Both players went on to play for the Youth Sports Federation of Nigeria (YSFON), Lagos State Academicals, Flying Eagles and Super Eagles.

4th Africa Cup of Nations, 11th March 1984, Bouake (Ivory Coast), Algeria – Nigeria (0-0). Nigeria's Green Eagles:
Standing: Ibrahim Danladi, Humphrey Edobor, Rasheed Yekini, Paul Okoku, Kingsley Paul, Peter Rufai, Stephen Keshi, Sunday Eboigbe and Wilfred Agbonabare
Sitting: Tarila Okorowanta, Mudashiru Lawal, Isa Shofoluwe, Clement Temile, Chibuzor Ehilegbu, Henry Nwosu and Bala Ali.

Stephen Keshi and Pele at the Stade El Menzah, Tunis, AFCON 1994. Paul Okoku was on the Nigerian Football Association team tagged Greater Tomorrow with Stephen Keshi when they travelled to Ibadan, in 1976, to meet with Pele of Brazil for his training camp for youth development sponsored by Pepsi company as their brand ambassador.

Flying Eagles, 1983 set with five players from St. Finbarr's College on the team, in the picture above are: Samson Siasia, Paul Okoku, Alphonsus Akhahon, Chris Anigala. Raymond King was missing from the picture.

Five players from St. Finbarr's College: Raymond King, Paul Okoku and Chris Anigala, missing from the picture were Samson Siasia and Alphonsus Akhahon. Flying Eagles team, 1983 set after presenting the Tesema trophy for the best U21 team in Africa to the late president of Nigeria, Alhaji Shehu Shagari, at the Dodan Barracks, the military barracks located in Ikoyi, Lagos, Nigeria.

Super Eagles players: Stephen Keshi and Paul Okoku in Rabat on the 28th of August 1983 against Morroco. Nigeria defeated Morocco on penalties 5-4.

Paul Okoku at the school boys' quarter.

Alabama A & M University players, Nathaniel Ogedegbe (captain) and Paul Okoku after a match against the University of Huntsville, (UAH) Alabama, 1985.

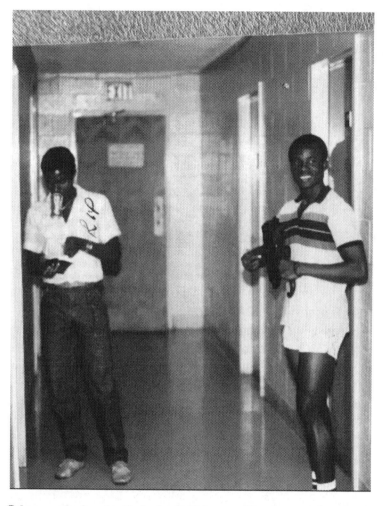

Obey Adedeji (aka Obey Reggae) and
Paul Okoku at the Hopkins Hall, (hostel),
Alabama A & M University, 1987

Five players from St. Finbarr's College: Raymond King, Paul Okoku and Chris Anigala, missing from the picture were Samson Siasia and Alphonsus Akhahon.
Flying Eagles team, 1983 set after presenting the Tesema trophy for the best U21 team in Africa to the late president of Nigeria, Alhaji Shehu Shagari, at the Dodan Barracks, the military barracks located in Ikoyi, Lagos, Nigeria.

St. Finbarr's College, 1981 set.
Standing, L - R: Steve Duru, Reserve goalkeeper (?), Chris Anigala,
Patrick Obitor, Idowu "Jencut" Abiodun, Godwin Etemere,
Raymond King and Sunday Joseph.
Squatting, L - R: Nojeem Farawe, John Itohan, Alphonsus
Akhahon, Ike, Dennis Echefu, Patrick Onyedeke and Paul Okoku.

The connection of the 1960's, 1970's, and the 1980's
Principal's Cup sensational of Saint Finbarr's College.
Great Conquerors! Left to right:
Emeka "Caterpillar" James, Paul Okoku, Bernard Senaya,
Emilio John, Nathaniel Ogedegbe (then president of
SFCOBA-America), Chris Oyobio, Virginius Amaechi
Nwogu, and Emmanuel Senaya.
SFCOBA Reunion, Dayton, Ohio, USA, August 17, 2019.

CHAPTER 6

NATHANIEL OGEDEGBE: FINBARR'S SOCCER GREAT

In 2013, ex-international Nathaniel Ogedegbe was inducted into the Hall of Fame in Huntsville, Alabama. He received several Resolutions and Proclamations from the State of Alabama, House of Representatives, County Commission, County of Madison and City of Huntsville, Alabama. Ogedegbe, who was recruited by Tim Hankinson, the then coach of the San Antonio Scorpions) to join the men's soccer program at Alabama A&M University. Since graduating from AAMU, Ogedegbe has remained active in soccer.

After having a stint with Worcester Wild Fire in the A League, Ogedegbe, also coached Hampshire College Amherst Massachusetts before starting his own brand of soccer program, Flawless Soccer in 1993.

A Civil Engineer by profession, Ogedegbe has worked for both private and public sectors as Airport Engineer at Galveston Municipal Airport, Assistant County Engineer with Franklin County Government, Engineer of Massachusetts Highway Department, Senior Engineer at CADD, Supervisor with City of Northampton Massachusetts, and presently Senior Engineer with the Town of Leesburg. Ogedegbe and his wife Erika have three children Benjamin Oritsebawo, Michaela Jolomi and Kayode. Benjamin graduated from Academy of Science and Tuscarora High school in 2013 and received a scholarship to play division one soccer at Indiana University and Perdue University Indianapolis.

CHAPTER 7

STEVEN KESHI: FINBARR'S SOCCER GREAT

On Oct 31, 2014, Stephen Keshi, a former Finbarr's soccer player was unceremoniously reappointed as Nigeria's soccer coach, only two weeks after the Nigeria Football Federation replaced him with Shaibu Amodu. Finbarr's world and, indeed, the sports world, were aghast by his replacement in the first place. So, much jubilation emerged following his reappointment. Some sports writers remained skeptical about the "new" promises made to Keshi. Below is one cautionary note presented by Author Sly Edaghese.

Keshi: Beware of That Greek Gift!
By
Sly Edaghese

Many might not have heard of the phrase Greek gift. Exactly, that's why I'm sounding the warning loud and clear to Mr Stephen Keshi, coach of the Nigerian national football team, the Super Eagles, to beware of "Greek gift."

On a meeting held last Tuesday by the NFA, Nigeria's football governing body, it was agreed by the board, though the agreement was far from being unanimous, that a 'Greek gift' be sent to Stephen Keshi. The Greek gift is a notification to be sent to the coach, who presently is holidaying with his family in the US, announcing the renewal of his contract of engagement with the Super Eagles.

I don't know if the official letter to renew Stephen Keshi's contract has got to him yet. But I'm sure his foot soldiers present at the venue of the meeting where the decision to reinstate him was made, must have called him to hint him of something good in the offing. Now if Keshi has received the letter, I want to tell him to reject it and throw it back at the face of the NFA. I realise how very crazy this would sound in the ears of the embattled coach, knowing how hard he had fought and how many buttons he had pressed to force the hand of the NFA to arrive at their latest decision. Yes, I realize all that. I also know when the present NFA chairman, Mr. Amaju Pinnick, who seems now to have made a volte face, openly snarled at the idea of renewing Stephen Keshi's contract, describing Keshi as a 'failed coach.' Now if this same man, who had repeatedly rebuffed several emissaries sent to him to endorse Keshi for a reappointment, suddenly turns around to become the one championing the cause of Keshi, I think a Greek gift must be in the making!

Now what's a Greek gift? A Greek gift is a gift with a colourful wrapping, like the colourful painting you see around the graves, whereas inside the belly of the so-called gift are poisonous snakes meant to put the receiver in a harm's way. The Greek gift originated in the war, according to legend, between Troy and Greece. The battle lasted for 10- years, no winner. The Greeks cunningly decided to play a fast one on the Trojans. What they did was to leave at the gate of Troy, the "Trojan Horse", which the Trojans, on seeing it, thought it was a parting gift left behind by the runaway cowardly Greeks who had given up on the war. The Trojans welcomed the gift and took it within their walls, little knowing the belly of the beast was laden with armed soldiers who would soon destroy their city. Stephen Keshi are you reading this. Beware! A word is enough for the wise. Happy New Year.

By Sly Edaghese, October 31, 2014

==

CHAPTER 8

CHRIS OYOBIO: FINBARR'S SOCCER GREAT

Photo of jubilating Father Slattery, Chris Oyobio, and Marcelus Obinatu after a Finbarr's soccer victory winning the championship Principal's Cup in 1972 against Baptist Academy High School. Oyobio is recognized as the icon of the championship game, the expert dribbler, and a great Finbarr's soccer player.

CHAPTER 9

GENERAL TESTIMONIALS
OF FINBARRIANS

R. T. N. ONYEJE
"What Rev. Fr. Slattery Taught Me"

I lost my parents at a tender age. As the Biblical saying goes, "Strike the Shepherd and the sheep will be scattered." At the demise of my parents, the children were scattered into different relations. Death robbed me of my parental guidance and counseling at an early age. The lot later fell on my eldest brother to take care of me; he became the beacon of my hope. Understandably, he was not well equipped by nature, being a man, to play the full role of parent. I must thank God, however, that his educational obligations towards me were religiously discharged. The usual fraternal relationship between brothers was missing because he was a devout believer in the maxim: "Spare the rod and spoil the child."

"An ideal environment for assimilating my true lessons of life was created when I got admitted into St. Finbarr's College when Rev. Fr. D.J. Slattery was the founding principal. While conducting his lessons on religious knowledge, he used to digress a great deal into diverse subjects such as Moral Ethics, Pilgrimage to the Holy Land, Dignity of Labor, Football, Hitler's submarines, and his aerial bombardments during the W.W. II, et cetera. I enjoyed and benefited tremendously from these digressions because it afforded me the opportunity to entrench in my young mind those values that would serve to improve the quality of my future life."

'From Father's speeches, sermons, reproaches, and commendations, he unwillingly taught me many edifying ways of life. He taught me that the youth would become the leaders of society. He would not entertain any alibi from me. He once pulled me by the shirt to lower my face to his level and buffeted and battered my face; short of giving me a black eye. He then fired, "One more report, and you are thrown through the corridor of no return." I was happy, however, because if Oga had not executed the punishment himself and decided to march me to his sergeant "Kolofo," Mr. "E," I would have cursed the day I was admitted into St. Finbarr's College. It would be of interest to know that Mr. "E," loved and applied the cane in a very forceful manner, with inexplicable delight. At the end of the "touch your toes" exercise, if you had any strength left in you to look up, you would notice a smile of ridicule on his countenance.

On Discipline and Honesty, Father taught me that one must be very disciplined and forthright before one could be called a disciplinarian and a leader. That was why discipline was the pivotal "sine qua non" at the school. During our days, if you were caught indulging in any fraudulent practice at the examination hall, you would have attracted to yourself an outright and irreversible expulsion. The West African Examinations Council was aware of the integrity and scrupulous honesty of the man at the helm of affairs at St. Finbarr's College (one would expect no less from a Catholic priest) and it wasted no time in granting formal approval for the college as center for its school certificate examination. Father did not condone any act of undisciplined behavior from his students, or even staff. If you were caught shabbily dressed in school uniform, even after school period, you would not go scot-free. Father also taught me that rules and regulations made for all, are not bent; they must be seen to apply to all and sundry.

Once you flagrantly broke any of the four commandments of the college, even if you were Pele of the college football team or the grade one prospect of an impending external examination, boy, you were a goner. You would be marshaled through the dreaded "corridor." No mercy, no "Egunje."

In conclusion, I am deeply grateful to Father Slattery for his positive influence on my life and the lives of all others who providentially received their spiritual and moral growth from him. My fellow retired conquerors who I spoke with attested to the prominent level of discipline that Father had implanted in their young lives, which they have been striving to live up to. We all love you, Father. I thank you immensely, Rev. Fr. Dennis Joseph Slattery, for everything.

F. B. A. OGUNDIPE

"St. Paul's School Apapa Road Sports Field – A Handiwork of Rev. Fr. D. J. Slattery"

Besides founding Saint Finbarr's College in the year 1956, the name of very Rev. Fr. D.J. Slattery is linked with the founding of other institutions such as SS Peter & Paul Somolu, St. Gabriel, Bariga, St. Dennis, Akoka, St. Flavious, Oworonsoki, etc., to mention a few. However, the deep involvement of this clergy/football administrator would not have been completed without mentioning a sports field constructed by him.

As already established, St. Finbarr's College was opened on Tuesday, January 10th, 1956, and it could be rightly said that playing of the game of football commenced simultaneously. The premises being used were St. Paul's Primary School, Apapa Road, our old or borrowed site. The field was very bushy and thorny and as such accommodated some dangerous reptiles and even scorpions in the water-logged zones.

The type of ball played by us at that time was either a tennis ball or Olympia popularly called "Bombom." These two balls would bounce well in the thick and uncleared field, nevertheless, the enthusiasm of the soccer-loving pioneers made the founding principal Rev. Fr. Slattery to think about the idea of transforming this thick bush into a befitting football/sports field. The uppermost was the thought that one day this might be useful in setting up a mini sports field which would stand the test of time for all to come. This field later became St. Paul's football ground Apapa Road, Ebute Metta.

Sometime around 1996, I happened to pass by St. Paul's School Apapa Road, when I saw a mammoth crowd watching a football match. I, being a football enthusiast myself, was eager to join the spectators, not only to watch the match but to see what changes or changes that might have taken place after some forty years that we left Apapa Road. Many structures have sprung up here and there in addition to the twenty-room apartment that we used to know. I also noticed the five classrooms given to us by our host, St. Paul's School, through the then Manager Rev. Fr. Florence Macathy S.M.A., which served as classrooms, staff room, bookstore, clerk's office, and the principal's living rooms. The field looks the same as it did in 1956. How did Fr. Slattery achieve this? He achieved this within a span of four months. First, he quickly organized a general manual labor daily for all the students. The first two weeks of our resumption was spent in clearing the proposed field and this period tallied with the Queen's visit to Nigeria in January 1956. St. Finbarr's College with number 162, was to take part in the Youth Week Parade slated for Saturday, February 11th, 1956. Within a fortnight, the surroundings of the field had been completed and we were privileged to use it in preparation for the match-past with a police officer in attendance.

The school went on a short vacation during the Queen's visit to reopen again on Monday, February 13th, 1956. Clearing of the field now became a regular exercise and as a punishment for erring pupils. The first two pupils to serve such punishment were masters Chike Igbonoba and Albert Jemade. These two refused to sweep the classroom after closing hours as ordered by the class prefect, Sylvester Ogunamana. At that time, the class prefect reported the case to the principal, who surprised everybody by announcing the dismissal of these two students. He later rescinded his decision by ordering the sentence of two weeks manual labor which would result in them clearing a quarter of the field. Moreover, because the Easter examination was near, they were to spend the holiday serving their punishment.

When school resumed for the second term on Monday May 7th, 1956, a quarter of the field had been cleared in addition to the surroundings. Manual labor was extended to two hours daily and the fear of being expelled for not obeying the principal's order was instilled in us. So, "afraid" was the watch word under the supervision of our class master, Mr. Ferdinand Ejieke. Before we knew what we were doing, within a short spate of time, the whole area was cleared, all the unwanted personnel removed, thick grass uprooted, bald portions were covered with Bahama grass and watered regularly. Thus, towards the end of May, the field was ready for marking, the rain helping us indeed. At last, there was the signpost of "Keep Off the Grass" meaning a sports field was in the making. The field looked beautiful and safe for use. The undulating portions were leveled.

Two factors contributed immensely to the development of the sports field indeed. These were some sporting equipment obtained from the then NFA. In 1955, the popular King George stadium, now Onikan Stadium, was to be expanded and fitted with modern amenities. The old wooden goalposts were to be replaced with aluminum types. All the old items removed from the stadium were given to charity. St. Finbarr's College was one of such beneficiaries. We gained the whole field equipment from the corner flags to the wooden goalpost and the nettings.

Also in that same year, 1955, at the Accra Sports Stadium, the Ghana Black Stars in the presence of Dr. Kwame Osaghefo Nkrumah spanked the Nigerian Red Devils by seven goals to nothing. This was the worst defeat ever suffered by our National Football Team. This sounds incredible but it is true, and this worst soccer defeat suffered by our National Team caused the then NFA officials to be disbanded, so also were the players. The jerseys used were considered to have been soiled by that tally and were not to be worn again.

Ghana proudly fielded stars like goalkeeper Layea, skipper Braindt Dogo Moro, Obilitey, Adjei, Adu Odamatey, Salisu, Baba Yara, Acqua, Aggrey Finn, Ofei Dodo, Ghamfi, and others. These were great names in the fifties and that defeat meted to Nigeria made St. Finbarr's College to inherit those jerseys. Eventually, the name Red Devil was changed to Green Eagles before it was finally changed to the present Super Eagles. Those red jerseys were used for practice.

With the provision of all the necessary equipment, white paints and lime were provided for the painting and marking of the field. The field looked as if it was being prepared for a big football match. This was the birth of the St. Paul's Ground. This is one of the dreams of Very Rev. Fr. D. J. Slattery, unknown to many people.

The field was officially opened on Friday June 29th, 1956, which was the first day of St. Paul's Primary School. A football match was arranged between the host, St. Paul's and the tenant St. Finbarr's College, which resulted in a 2 – 1 win for the host.

The construction of the field was a great delight to the Headmaster of the St. Paul's school, Mr. Shote and Fr. McCarthy, the manager. The field served a dual purpose that is, as a football and an athletics field, and both pupils of St. Paul's Primary School and St. Finbarr's College benefited tremendously from it. However, it is on record that we did not play any other match on this ground until we left finally for Akoka in January 1959. This was simply because we were playing away matches to selected teams like St. Gregory's College, Obalende, St. Leo's Teachers, Training College Abeokuta, Eko Boys' High School, etc.

As for athletics, we had our first inter-house sports on the field on Tuesday September 25th, 1956. This continued every year until we finally moved to our Promised Land at Akoka.

SEGUN AJANLEKOKO
"The Rev. Father Slattery I Knew"

The Rev. Father Slattery I knew commenced in January 1965 when I gained admission into Form 1 at Saint Finbarr's College, Akoka. Then, the road that led to Saint Finbarr's College was most unimaginable, absolutely impassable terrain, and at the end of that long winding road you would find the pacesetter and beacon to the great upsurge in educational setting in Akoka, which SFC pioneered in those days before the like of Unilag, Our Lady of Apostles, and Anglican Boys Grammar School joined the educational match.

Rev. Father Slattery was a strict disciplinarian and very agile. I believe his stature and height (under 5ft tall) must have helped him to be able to move around very quickly. He was like a colossus in those days, yet he had an accommodating manner. There were certain things he could not stand. They were:

1. Tardiness
2. Untidiness
3. Mediocrity
4. Lies.

He was a quick-witted fellow and expected people that he had trained to be well at the top of their chosen professions.

Talking about lateness, I remember often, the story of "the last trip" (i.e., every day the school van did a round trip from Akoka to Yaba to bring students to the school three times in the morning). The last trip, which was the third one, comes at about 7:50 a.m. By the time the last trip came in and school morning assembly commenced, Father Slattery would be found lurking by the gate to the school waiting for latecomers. Usually, the students are very smart, so they too usually bid their time before coming in. But often this lurking practice was so elusive that you hardly knew where he was after morning assembly. I can remember that often he pounced on students and chased them as far as the present-day end of university road. Some he caught, some escaped. If you were caught, the Lord would help you!

His first punishment was a slap and then you were sent to VP and senior tutor who were experts at caning unruly students. More often, he sent people back home when they were late. Such was the fear that was instilled in those of us who were opportune to have tutelage under him that punctuality was one of the first lessons each one of us had to learn when we got into SFC.

Lateness did not end with students alone. I witnessed teachers being shouted at to go back home once they were late. In fact, it was imperative for the teachers to be at the assembly with the students. That was the order and discipline of those days! That was a great teacher, Father Slattery.

As for tidiness, the morning Assembly was really an opportunity after prayers for the Principal and Senior tutors to inspect students' class by class while standing on the college ground to look at how clean your white uniform was; whether the nails are cut, shoes checked to see if properly polished. For those who were adults (yes, we had some adult students in those days), they must be clean-shaven, school uniform must not be torn, and nails must not be in terrible state. If any of the students was found wanting in this regard, he was sent home to come back only when he had secured the proper attire.

Cleanliness and tidiness were a tall order that must be adhered to by the young ones in those days, when you consider the bad roads, they must pass through before getting to school; especially during rainy seasons when it is very muddy. Here we are, Father Slattery still held on to seeing us clean. Today, I can say, however, that this has rubbed off on us. I look down on people who are improperly dressed, as my perception of them goes down. I do not believe that you can be untidy and be responsible. Cleanliness is next to Godliness – that was the rule we were taught.

The consequences of not meeting with the standard expected by Father Slattery are:

- – Cutting grass
- – Kneeling for 1 hour with hands stretched up very wide.

Of course, in football, during our time, we won the coveted trophy called the Principal Cup 3 times out of our 5-year stay in the college. In 1968 and 1969 we won it back-to-back. The team was so good that four of them were called up (right from High School) to play for the National team - the Green Eagles; viz. Emilio John; Ajibade, Peter Egbiri and Richard Ibeh.

ACADEMIC PROWESS

However, one area, which often, people overlook about SFC, when they talk about our prowess in football, is academics. It is on record that in those days whoever did not pass the promotional exams got expelled. If you got to Form 5 in those days, you could rest assured that your WASC result would be good; for you would have passed through the screening process set up by Father Slattery.

In my own time, 65/69 set, we had the best result in the whole of Lagos State, next was Kings College. Out of eighty-five of us that sat for the WAEC, we had thirty-one grade ones. Proficiency in education was necessary if you wanted to be a friend of Father Slattery in those days, never mind being a very keen footballer.

For the record, the Rev. Father D. J. Slattery imbued in us steadfastness, diligence, faithfulness, and noble heartedness! That has helped a lot of Finbarrians to be where they are today. The like of Prof. Badiru, Prof. Eleshe, Prof. Sonubi, Vice Admiral Patrick Koshoni Nze mark Odu, Dr. Wole Adedeji and a whole lot of others.

DONATUS OGUAMANAM
"My Memory of Saint Finbarr's College"

Coming to St. Finbarr's College is one of the best decisions my parents ever made on my behalf. I was in Primary 5 when my parents started contemplating my secondary education. As at the time of the discourse, the list of schools, in order of preference, had St. Gregory, St. Finbarr's College, Igbobi College, CMS, Methodist Boys High School, and King's College. King's College was the last because my father felt that only the children of the "connected" and "influential" stood a chance.

Following their research, I would assume, the list narrowed to three with St. Finbarr's College, St. Gregory, and Igbobi College, in that order. Well, I passed the examination and came to St. Finbarr's with my father on the day for interview. I recollect seeing Father Slattery on that day, but I cannot remember any encounter with him. The interview comprised written and oral sessions. At a point during the interview, the interviewer wondered whether I would like to enroll into the technical or grammar program. The question was strange, and I implored the interviewer to excuse me a minute to consult with my father who immediately opted for grammar; so, began my story at St. Finbarr's.

Finbarr's was competitive. Finbarr's was fun. My first year was a disaster as I missed the top three spots. My confidence was shaken, but that would change in the subsequent years, thanks to my parents, my physics and mathematics teachers, and Father Slattery. I was a regular at Father Slattery's moral instruction class. There was no examination and grades were not awarded. One was, however, obligated to attend the sessions for numerous reasons.

The moral instruction session was a talk on current affairs, philosophy, theology, and sociology. In retrospect, it was aimed at imbibing ethical principles and strongly defining what it takes to be a Finbarrian. Thus, it is no surprise that the first session was on the history of the College. It was in moral instruction class that I first came across the difference between failure and success. The former, if I may paraphrase the blessed Father, is the one who has not risen from the last fall, while the latter is one who has risen one more than the falls.

We were told to depend less on others and more on our abilities. This is in accord with one of the school's four pillars: that one should fail honorably as opposed to passing dishonorably, i.e., by cheating. Hence, it was common to find rooms where an examination was being conducted to be momentarily without invigilator(s).

Father Slattery was proud of his accomplishments at St. Finbarr's College then and was even prouder of his plans for the future of the school. He spoke very passionately about the progress of the college considering its short existence vis-à-vis the other older schools. He was convinced that Finbarr's had to be the best and Finbarr's was the best. His passion explains the agony he felt when he gave his swan song moral instruction class.

Father Slattery was not a happy man when the Lagos State government, under the governorship of Alhaji Lateef Jakande, in its wisdom decided to assume ownership of St. Finbarr's College and the rest of the Mission Schools. It is my view that he must have underestimated the intent of the government and decided to persevere until it became very lucid that there was little anyone could do about the development. Father left Finbarr's brokenhearted, stressing that one never made the weak strong by making the strong weak. This view has now been vindicated by time.

Mr. Kpotie was the principal when Father Slattery finally stopped holding moral instruction sessions. I was known to Mr. Kpotie for all the right reasons. However, I was caught outside school during break on my way to West African Examination Council's (WAEC) at Fadeyi. I was walking down the college road, heading towards the University of Lagos gate, reflecting on university life, when I was jolted to reality by voices from a car that had stopped beside me. Turning in the direction of the voices, I froze in the recognition of Father Slattery and Mr. Kpotie. They, and another teacher, were riding in Mr. Kpotie's car.

Being conversant with the rules of the school, I knew my fate and was wondering how I could write my examinations as an independent student since I am going to be expelled and I might not find admission in a comparable school. I was ushered into the car, and nobody spoke a word to me until we arrived at the college. At this point Mr. Kpotie wanted to know what I was doing outside in complete school's uniform (I was wearing my cardigan) while Father Slattery, the martinet, watched.

I was in Class four, and I told them that my parents wanted me to take the General Certificate of Education (GCE) examination in preparation for Class five's WAEC examination. I showed them the form I was going to submit and informed them that my parents were aware that I was going to submit the form during the break period because I come to school at about 7:00 a.m. and get home late because I go to private lessons immediately after school. To my surprise, Father Slattery went into a discourse with Mr. Kpotie who directed me afterwards to undergo some punishments.

The joy that overwhelmed me by this singular act of kindness on the part of Father Slattery is ineffable. While I cannot explain this act, it is plausible to conjecture that he believed the veracity of my narration and considered my academic record. Whatever it may be, I remain eternally grateful.

I cannot remember all the stories from Father Slattery's moral instruction sessions, but the fundamental principles are still etched in my memory. Father Slattery, via the founding and excellent management of St. Finbarr's College, touched and is still touching many. I left college with the tools to take on the world: a strong-willed but compassionate heart, a disciplined and prayerful mind, and a sound education.

In closing, I must mention that Finbarr's was so self-sufficient in experimental apparatus, especially basic things like potentiometer and rheostat that could easily be fabricated by the technical students and their supervisors, that the school supplied other schools during WAEC examinations. That was made possible by the foresight of Father Slattery.

DR. JOHN NWOFIA
"My Saint Finbarr's College Experience"

It was with excitement and trepidation that I showed up for my first day in 1975 from one class. I had chosen to be in the technical section. I showed up embarrassingly with my father who felt I should not limit myself and had me transferred to the Grammar section. Before we met with him, I had watched this sprightly, smiling man in the priestly robe with his cane ushering parents and, obviously, new students, to different teachers who had assembled in front of the academic staff room. We later met Father Slattery and he effected the change for me. He personally walked me to my new classroom, Form 1B. We saw a lot of Fr. Slattery in our first year. Our class was on the ground floor of the library building, which itself was directly adjacent to the staff room. We found out, soon enough, that we could not be rowdy in class without Fr. Slattery being aware. The lesson of the first few unlucky students was enough. It was in that first year that I saw how a smiling priest could wield his stick sternly but still be regarded fondly by all, even the students whose rear ends were still smarting from the stick.

We were all disappointed when the Gov. Jakande government waded into Missionary schools and took over. Father Slattery was relieved of his post as principal but remained as the Moral Instruction teacher. In the classes one could hear his frustration as he could only watch his beloved school sliding into mediocrity under government control. He would tell the story of his sojourn in Nigeria, how he founded the school, his roles in the Nigerian Football Association. Some of his best stories centered around history of the closeness and adversity (from football) between St Finbarr's College (SFC) and St. Gregory's College. It was ironical that Mr. Anthony Omoera (deceased) had been drafted from St. Gregory's to be Fr. Slattery's replacement at SFC.

The former Vice Principal, Mr. Kpotie, soon took over from Mr. Omoera as principal. We initially saw a bit of Fr. Slattery's style of management, but this quickly disappeared to his own personal style. My year was unique as the last group to be welcomed by the Rev. Fr. Denis J Slattery to SFC. We remain forever grateful for that privilege. As we celebrate our Silver

Jubilee (Class of 1975/1980) we will honor the man whom we loved and feared, our parents respected and adored. It is easy to guess that over ninety percent of the students at SFC came in because of Fr. Slattery's style of discipline which was responsible for the achievement of the school in the West African School Certificate (WASC) examinations and in the principal's cup football competition. SFC was synonymous with Fr. Slattery. You could not mention one without the other

Fr. Slattery treated every student equally. He did not care whether you were the Army General's son or the son of the driver. I personally witnessed him ordering out of his office an Army Captain who wanted his son, who did not score high enough in the Common Entrance Examination, admitted to the school. He did not care about the threats from the army officer. That was the style and courage of Fr. Slattery.

PHILIP BIENI
"Oga Taught Us Hard Work"

Oga, as we called him, will always remain a hero to all Finbarians. He taught us about demanding work, persistence, prioritizing, and quality management of all our endeavors. He also inspired us to treat others as we would like to be treated. Oga always respected other religious groups. During our school days, he made duty for all Muslims to leave school at noon on Fridays for their prayer meetings at the mosque. He always maintained that all humans are equal in the eyes of God. My series of conversations with him at his convent in Ireland before his death. He told me how proud he was of all the achievements of all his boys all over the world. He added that he looks forward to going back to Nigeria as his final resting place. be highly missed. May his soul rest in perfect peace.

CHAPTER 10

MY OWN SOCCER SOJOURN

Although I played on the Mosquitos and Rabits developmental soccer teams at Finbarr's in 1968/1969, I never rose to the level of playing for Finbarr's competitively-selected teams. I guess I guess I had only the academics and discipline portions of a complete Finbarrian. Two out of three is not bad. ☺ But I did have a true love of the game, even if the Finbarr's-level skills were lacking.

The famed sportscasters, Howard Cossell and Jim McKay were noted for popularizing the following quote:

"The joy of victory and the agony of defeat."

Luckily, when the agony of defeat does occur, people still play the game for the love of the game and the fun of playing. That was the case with me. I remember the painful losses in the few developmental soccer games I played for Finbarr's against Saint Gregory's College (Obalende, Lagos). Outside of Finbarr's, I have continued to embrace the love of soccer for many decades. In my neighborhood of Ebute-Metta, Lagos, I organized a rag-tag neighborhood soccer team named Afro-Melody Football Club in 1970. I was the organizer, the coach, and a player on the team. I even issued identification cards for the team members.

We played ad-hoc games against equally rag tag teams around the mainland of Lagos, including Shomolu, Apapa, Agege, Bariga, and others. With mixed game successes and a lack of a sponsor, the club eventually fizzled out. But my love of the game continued and led to my life-long dedication to the topic of soccer, mostly to align myself with the Finbarr's legacy of soccer supremacy. Therein lies the description of my post-Finbarr's soccer affiliation as a sojourn.

Upon arriving in the USA for further studies, I played on the soccer team for Tennessee Technological University in 1976/1977. Between 1982 and 1984, I also played on a recreational soccer team in Orlando, Florida.

Soccer Team of Tennessee Technological University,
Cookeville, Tennessee (1977)

Later, in the 1990s, I served as a coach and player for an adult soccer team, **The Crusaders**, in Norman, Oklahoma, with exceptional successes, as documented by several newspaper articles. I also coached youth soccer, with admirable results, which I credit to my Saint Finbarr's College background.

The Crusaders Adult Soccer Team, Norman, Oklahoma, 1994

The Norman (Okla.) Transcript, Tuesday, May 6, 1997   13

DRAGONS UNDEFEATED

Monroe Dragons 6 COED soccer team went undefeated during spring regular season play with a 7-0 record. The team beat regular-season opponents by a margin of 84-25. Team members include: Tunji Badiru, Scott Hanna-Riggs, Hunter Madole, Blake Smith, Nick Suit, and Chelsey Womack. The team is coached by Deji Badiru.

==

The Norman (Okla.) Transcript, Thursday, October 6, 1974   13

CRUSADERS IMPALE IMPACT

The Norman Crusaders defeated the Oklahoma City Impact last weekend in Central Oklahoma Adult Soccer League action at Whittier Middle School. David Morse scored two goals and Ernie Terrell, Emmanuel Akande and John Masango each had one. David Bolfrey dished out two assists and Miguel Grijalva had one assist and played steady defense in support of goalkeepers Craig Nelson and Chris Lajuwomi. The Crusaders, now 4-0, play defending state champion, Oklahoma City Soccer Center, Sunday at Macfarland Park. The Crusaders are coached by coach-player Deji Badiru.

==

14   The Norman (Okla.) Transcript, Friday, October 14, 1994

CRUSADERS TIE STATE CHAMPS

OKLAHOMA CITY -- The Norman Crusaders tied the defending state champion Soccer Center 3-3 Sunday at MacFarland Park in the Central Oklahoma Adult Soccer League. David Bolfrey and John Nash Masango scored goals.

==

The Norman (Okla.) Transcript, Friday, October 18, 1994 13

CRUSADERS STILL UNBEATEN

The Norman Crusaders defeated the Oklahoma City Intruders 6-1 Sunday in Central Oklahoma Adult Soccer League action at Whittier Middle

School. John Nash Masango scored two goals and Ade Okewole, David Morse, David Bolfrey and Miguel Grijalva also scored for the Crusaders, 5-0-1. Bolfrey and Ernie Terrel had assists while Emmanuel Akande, Mike Tonubbee and Manuel Aguilar provide stout defense to support Craig Nelson's goaltending. Crusaders coach is Deji Badiru.

==

The Norman (Okla.) Transcript, Tuesday, October 25, 1994 15

CRUSADERS SCALD CITY HEAT

The Norman Crusaders defeated City Heat 4-1 last weekend in Central Oklahoma Adult Soccer League play at Whittier Middle School. David Bolfrey scored two goals and Ernie Terrel and Randy Venk each scored one. Deji Badiru had an assist while Craig Nelson and Nash Masango shared time as goalkeepers. Bob Byers, Ed Bonzie, Miguel Grijalva and Al Larsen also turned in strong play for the Crusaders, 6-0-1.

==

16 The Norman (Okla.) Transcript, Wed, November 2, 1994

CRUSADERS TRIM VISTA

The Norman Crusaders Soccer Club defeated Vista 4-1 last weekend in Central Oklahoma Adult Soccer League play at Whittier Middle School. Ade Okewole scored two goals for the Crusaders, now 7-0-1. Nash Masango and Ed Bonzie each scored one. Doug Reimer turned in a solid performance both as sweeper and back-up goalie for Craig Nelson.

Mike Tonubbee, Manny Aguilar, Miguel Grijalva and Emmanuel Akande played strong defense. Deji Badiru is coach-player for the Crusaders.

===

The Norman (Okla.) Transcript, Monday, November 7, 1994 17

CRUSADERS CLAIM TITLE

The Norman Crusaders defeated Soccer Center 6-3 Sunday to capture the Central Oklahoma Adult Soccer League Title for the second time in three years. David Bolfrey and Ade Okewole each scored two goals and Ernie Terrell and Emmanuel Akande each had one goal. Molua Lambe, Chris Lajuwomi, David Morse and Nash Masango contributed assists for the Crusaders (8-0-1), who had been tied earlier in the season by Soccer Center. Akande, Manuel Aguilar, Mike Tonubbee and Doug Reimer played solid defense while Ed Bonzie, Bob Byers, Miguel Grijalva, Randy Venk and coach-player Deji Badiru excelled at midfield. Goalie Craig Nelson added several spectacular saves.

===

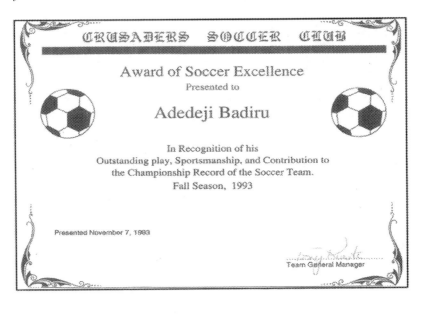

===

The Norman (Okla.) Transcript, Thursday, March 16, 1995 15

CRUSADERS OPEN WITH WIN

The Norman Crusaders adult soccer team opened the season with an 11-0 victory over Impact. Brent Maze and Nash Masango scored three goals, Ernie Terrell scored two and Ade Okewole, Shelly Lambe and Miguel Grijalva each scored once. Jim Rice, Emmanuel Akande played solid defense and Craig Nelson posted the shutout. The team is coached by Deji Badiru.

===

The Norman (Okla.) Transcript, Tuesday, March 28, 1995 13

CRUSADERS COOL OFF HEAT

The Norman Crusaders defeated City Heat 4-2 Sunday in Central Oklahoma Adult Soccer League play. Ernie Terrell scored two goals. Ade Okewole and David Bolfrey each scored one goal. Emmanuel Akande, Jim Rice, Mike Tonubbee, Manny Aguilar and goalie Craig Nelson paced the defense for Coach-player Deji Badiru's Crusaders.

==

16 The Norman (Okla.) Transcript, Thursday, April 6, 1995

CRUSADERS EDGE LIBERTY

The Norman Crusaders defeated Liberty 4-2 Sunday in Central Oklahoma Adult Soccer League play. Nash Masango scored two goals while Brent Maze and Reza Khakpour each tallied once. David Bolfrey and Ade Okewole each had an assist. Shelly Lambe, Ernie Terrell and David Morse played strong on defense. Emmanuel Akande, Manny Aguilar, Mike Tonubbee, Randy Venk, Doug Reimer and Miguel Grijalva shined on defense and goalie Craig Nelson made several spectacular saves to preserve the win. The Crusaders, the defending season champs, are coached by Deji Badiru.

==

The Norman (Okla.) Transcript, Tuesday, April 11, 1995 13

CRUSADERS DUMP INTRUDERS

The Norman Crusaders defeated the Intruders 5-2 Sunday in Central Oklahoma Adult Soccer League action. Pato Morales, Shelly Lambe, Chris Lajuwomi, Reza Khakpour and David Morse scored goals for the Crusaders. Ade Okewole had two assists. Coach-player Deji Badiru, Miguel Grijalva, Randy Venk, Al Larsen, Nash Masango, Ernie Terrell, Jim Rice and goalie Craig Nelson also played well.

===

Well, to prove that everything good comes to an end at some point, even with a good coach-player, the championship reign of the Crusaders Adult Soccer team came to an end in May 1995; as documented by the league's news account below:

"The Norman Crusaders Soccer Club lost 2-4 to Pyramid Soccer Club on Sunday, May 14 in the season playoffs of the Central Oklahoma Adult Soccer league. Coach-player Deji Badiru and Ade Okewole each scored one goal for the Crusaders. Emmanuel Akande, Jim Rice, Manny Aguilar, and Mike Tonubbee played hard on defense. Ernie Terrell, David Morse, Pato Morales, Reza Khakpour, Bob Byers, Miguel Grijalva, Al Larsen and Pato Morales all played very strong. Craig Nelson played strong in goal. The play-off games continue Sunday at North Oklahoma City soccer complex." This finale demonstrates the joy of victory and the agony of defeat.

MY PHYSICS OF SOCCER WEBSITE

All my soccer love affairs culminated in my development of the Physics of Website, www.physicsofsoccer.com, which is dedicated to teaching kids how to leverage math and science to improve their soccer games. Readers are encouraged to visit the website.

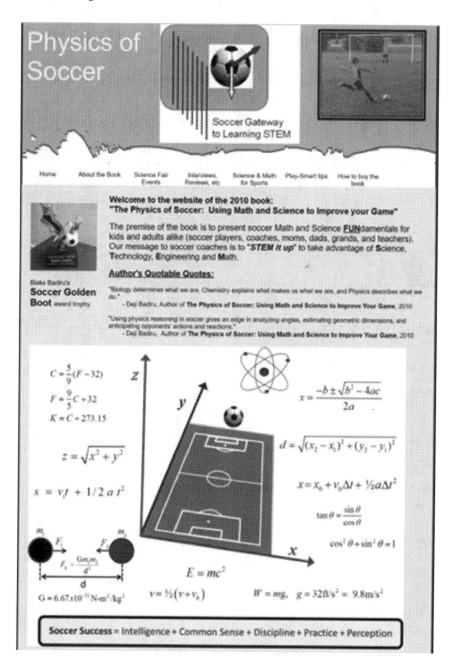

Soccer is a family affair in the Badiru household. Everybody is involved in one role or another, as we push the message of science, technology, engineering, and mathematics (STEM) in youth communities.

In coaching the Adult soccer team, I did call upon my Finbarr's heritage of academics and discipline by executing the coaching from an intellectual perspective rather than the conventional sports perspective. I applied the principle of scientific management, as narrative in the following paragraphs.

SCIENTIFIC MANAGEMENT OF A SOCCER TEAM

Soccer game management is as important as any other field of management in business and industry. The concepts of scientific management are also applicable to managing a soccer team. As a soccer coach-player in the early 1990's, the author applied his professional management skills to developing a process for total game management on and off the soccer playing field.

Management principles and discipline instilled by the technique of total quality management (TQM) can be used to improve any process ranging from recreational activities to professional endeavors.

In the business world, the concepts of lean and Six Sigma are used to improve process and procedures for accomplishing work. These same concepts can be applied to the business of soccer management. Training management, game execution management, and soccer organization management can benefit from lean and Six Sigma techniques.

CONCEPT OF SIX SIGMA FOR SOCCER

The Six Sigma approach, which was originally introduced by Motorola's Government Electronics Group, has caught on quickly in business and industry. Many major companies now embrace the approach as the key to high quality business productivity. Six Sigma means six standard deviations from a statistical performance average. The Six Sigma approach allows for no more than 3.4 defects per million parts in manufactured goods or 3.4 mistakes per million activities in a service operation. To appreciate the effect of the Six Sigma approach, consider a process that is 99% perfect. That process will produce 10,000 defects per million parts. With Six Sigma, the process will need to be 99.99966% perfect in order to produce only 3.4 defects per million. Thus, Six Sigma is an approach that pushes the limit of perfection.

The technique of Six Sigma uses statistical methods to find problems that cause defects so that they can be corrected. For example, the total yield (number of non-defective units) from a process is determined by a combination of the performance levels of all the steps making up the process. If a process consists of 20 steps and each step is 98% perfect, then the performance of the overall process will be:

$$(0.98)^{20} = 0.667608 \text{ (i.e., } 66.7608\%)$$

Thus, the process will produce 332,392 defects per million parts. If each step of the process is pushed to the Six Sigma limit, then the process performance will have the following composite performance level:

$$(0.9999966)^{20} = 0.999932 \text{ (i.e. } 99.9932\%)$$

Based on the above calculation, the Six Sigma process will produce only 68 defects per million parts. This is a significant improvement over the original process performance. In many cases, it is not realistic to expect to achieve the Six Sigma level of production. But the approach helps to set a quality standard and provides a mechanism for striving to reach the target goal. In effect, the Six Sigma process means changing the way workers perform their tasks so as to minimize the potential for defects.

CONCEPT OF LEAN PROCESS FOR SOCCER

What is "lean?" Lean means the identification and elimination of sources of *waste* in operations. Recall that Six Sigma involves the identification and elimination of sources of *defects*. When lean and Six Sigma are combined, an organization can achieve the double benefit of reducing waste and defects in operations, which leads to what is known as lean Six Sigma. Consequently, the organization can achieve higher product quality, better employee morale, better satisfaction of customer requirements, and more effective utilization of limited resources. The basic principle of "lean" is to take a close look at the elemental compositions of a process so that non-value-adding elements (or movements) can be located and eliminated. Both lean and Six Sigma use analytical and statistical techniques as the basis for pursuing improvement objectives. But the achievement of those goals depends on having a structured approach to the activities associated with what needs to be done.

If proper project management is embraced at the outset in a soccer management endeavor, it will pave the way for achieving Six Sigma results and make it possible to realize lean outcomes. The key in any soccer management endeavor is to have a structured plan of the soccer project so that diagnostic and corrective steps can be pursued. If the proverbial "garbage" is allowed to creep into a soccer effort, it would take much more time, effort, and cost to achieve a lean Six Sigma cleanup.

To put the above concepts in a soccer perspective, Six Sigma implies conducting soccer practice such that errors are minimized in the long run. Likewise, the technique of lean ensures that only value-adding movements are made during practice and game execution. For example, the ability to pass the ball within close quarters on the soccer field is highly coveted and requires hours and hours of practice. When it becomes like second nature, it can be done intuitively. An analogy for lean Six Sigma application to soccer movement relates to the concept of being within or outside the specification limits. If practice involves moving the ball within close confines, then Six Sigma means the ability to consistently keep the ball within specification (specs) limits. Balls falling outside specs limit do not meet "quality" requirements. That means they fall outside specs. In applying lean concept approach, being able to keep the ball close means avoiding and eliminating unnecessary motions. This means the elimination of waste.

I have a personal experience in the application of the concepts of TQM process in coaching an adult soccer team. I served as the coach of an adult recreational soccer team in 1992-1994 in the Central Oklahoma Adult Soccer League (COASL). Using TQM processes, I took the team from being at the bottom of the league to being the league champion in just three seasons. This was not due to my coaching acumen, but rather, the way I motivated the team and made everyone aware of his respective responsibilities on the team on and off the field.

As a coach-player, I applied TQM techniques to the way I handled team assignments and encouraged the other players to do likewise. I developed a documentation system that, each week, informed the players of where the team stood in relation to other teams. Each week, I handed out written notes about what the current objectives were and how they would be addressed. Because of this, I was nicknamed "Memo Coach" because of the frequent written memos that I gave to players. It got to a point where the players got used to being given written assignments, and they would jokingly demand their memo for the week. Copies of graphical representation of the game lineup were given to the players to study prior to each game. Each person had to know his immediate coordination points during a game: who would provide support for whom, who would cover what area of the field, and so on. I applied TQM to various aspects of the team, including and following:

- Team registration
- Team motivation
- Team communication
- Team cooperation
- Team coordination
- Expected individual commitment
- Player camaraderie
- Field preparation
- Sportsmanship
- Play etiquette
- Game lineup
- Training regimen
- Funding

Everybody had an assignment that was explained and coordinated from the standpoint of total team and game management. In the second season under this unconventional coaching method, the team took third place. The players were all excited and motivated and credited the success to the way the management of the team was handled. So, starting the third season, everyone came out highly charged up to move the team forward to an even better season. Of course, there was the season's inaugural memo waiting for the team.

One of the favorite memos handed out to the team was the one that indicated the team's track record (Win-Lose-Draw) dating back 10 years. With this, I was able to motivate the team that it was time to move to the next higher level in the league. Traditionally, the team has been viewed as one of the "so-so" teams in the league. Not a bad team, but not among the elite. I convinced the players that while winning was not everything (particularly in an adult soccer league), it sure would feel better than losing. This was in an "over-30" league, tactfully referred to as the Masters League, where most of the players were technical or business professionals.

With the high level of motivation, division of labor, and effective utilization of existing resources (soccer skills, or lack thereof), the team was crowned the league champion in Fall 1993. This is not a small feat in a league that contained traditional powerhouses. It is interesting to note that the achievement was made with little or no recruitment of additional "skillful" players, who were in short supply anyway in that league at that time. This shows that with proper management, existing resources of a team can be leveraged to achieve an unprecedented level of improvement both in direct skills development as well as total team and game management. In particular, using the techniques of project management for soccer management has many advantages including the following:

- Better connection with other players
- More traceable lines of communication
- More sustainable levels of cooperation
- Better pathways of coordination
- Holistic systems view of soccer game scenarios

In this case example, Finbarr's academics and discipline helped to facilitate sports excellence.

DON'T DROP THE BALL, FIGURATIVELY

Whether you are a player, coach, parent, referee, or league administrator, don't drop the ball when it comes to crucial affairs of soccer as demonstrated by my case study above. A coach must use total team management, as in total quality management, to avoid dropping the ball.

CONCLUSION

I hope this journey into the legacy of Saint Finbarr's College has been exciting and informative for all readers. The trifecta of Academics, Discipline, and Sports (specifically, soccer) has paved the way for multidimensional career and professional accomplishments of Finbarrians. The Boys of Finbarr's have gone on to serve the broad society.

REFERENCES FOR CHAPTER 10

1. Badiru, Deji (2022), **More Physics of Soccer: Playing the Game Smart and Safe**, iUniverse, Bloomington, Indiana, 2022.
2. Badiru, Deji (2018), *The Story of Saint Finbarr's College: Father Slattery's Contributions to Education and Sports in Nigeria*, iUniverse, Bloomington, Indiana, USA, 2018
3. Badiru, Deji (2018), *Physics of Soccer II: Science and Strategies for a Better Game*, iUniverse, Bloomington, Indiana, USA, 2018
4. Badiru, Deji (2014), *Youth Soccer Training Slides: A Math and Science Approach*, iUniverse, Bloomington, Indiana, USA, 2014
5. Badiru, Deji (2010), *Physics of Soccer: Using Math and Science to Improve Your Game*, iUniverse, Bloomington, Indiana, USA, 2010

APPENDIX A

TRIBUTE TO BERNARD SENAYA BY JOHN SENAYA

THE LIFE AND TIMES OF BERNARD KWAKU SENAYA
JULY 12, 1950 – DECEMBER 5, 2022

Saying he had an uncommon obsession for timekeeping would be an understatement. Simply put, Bernard Kwakwu Senaya never, ever joked about appointments... not even the most informal. He simply was a stickler for time.

Up until his passing, he would, one day ahead, have arranged all he needed for the next day's appointment, clothes, shoes, underwear...all neatly set aside. Today, he most certainly is keeping up his appointment with the Almighty Father...at the appointed time.

Bernard Kwaku Senaya, the second of five sons and one beautiful daughter of Vivian and Irene Senaya, was born in Ebute Metta, Lagos on Wednesday the 12th of July 1950. His parents, Vivian, and Irene were themselves practical examples of humility, discipline, kindness, and respect for all; but young Bernard (better referred to as Aku in those days) made these virtues his, in a most unique, outstanding, life-long way. Ladi Lak Institute, in the heart of Ebute Metta, Lagos was his first formal educational port of call between 1957 to 1963.

From that point, his unusual athleticism on the sports field started showing up. He was even rumored to have always gone to bed every night with his football. And, why not? Soccer was to become his banner for life. Bernard became the most sought-after football star in the community he grew up in; especially the schools he attended.

From the Lagos Secondary Commercial Academy, Yaba, where he continued his education from 1964 to 1968, he was poached by Late Anthony Omoera, then Vice Principal of St. Finbarr's College Akoka to join the "deadliest" schoolboy soccer team in 1968 to initiate what later became The Akoka Conquerors.

This became the springboard for Bernard's stardom which resonated across Lagos State, nationally and internationally. He was instrumental to the winning of the "Principal's Cup" both in 1968 and in 1969 He joined St Finbarr's College, Akoka in 1968 to 1970 and those were the years when Bernard Senaya together with his team mates-Emilio John, Peter Egbiri, Thomas Iweibo, George Akhigbe ravaged every opposing team with never-to-be-equaled freedom and impact that etched the name St. Finbarr's in gold, up till today.

Even the family name-Senaya-became synonymous with soccer because of Bernard's achievements on the pitch. Many who never met him at St. Finbarr's, at least heard about him and felt the impact of his devastating meanness on the field.

He was a notable businessman in front of goal and was known to never celebrate after scoring goals focusing on retrieving the ball from the net and getting back to business. On one occasion, Bernard led his school team in a 13-nil routing of this younger brother, Kwame's school team, Yabatech ...led him back home, without apologies! Some sins are never forgiven!

One would imagine that his ruthlessness on the pitch would make him feared, off the pitch; On the contrary, Bernard was always that cool, calm, respectable, respectful, ever-loving, ever-smiling, warm, always-ready-to-help and ever-contented, father, brother, and friend. Bernard served as Chairman St Finbarr's College Class of 1966-1970 set and also as National President of the St Finbarr's Old Boys Association (SFCOBA) from 1999 to 2002 Growing up, Bernard was most supportive with house chores; always being the one to diligently and painstakingly carry out all the chores, setting the highest standards in performance and consistency within the family.

Bernard was the gemstone when it came to doing things right.

No doubt, it became difficult for Bernard to hide his qualities from sports poachers which resulted to him being given the Beacon of Light Award in 2019 by the US branch of St Finbarr's Old Boys Association (SFCOBA) in Dayton, Ohio, USA The young man was quickly snapped up in 1971 by the Nigeria Airways (then W.A.A.C) by the team manager, Peter Eruteya who made sure he got him to lead the attack in his team, devastating several bigger names in the soccer league, at that time consisting of the likes of E.C.N.(NEPA), Stationery Stores, Leventis, Nigeria Police and others. He played alongside the likes of Peter and Paul Baby Anieke, Joe Eriko, Tunde Martins, and a host of others.

Soccer laid the foundation for Bernard's professional life. In 1978, he moved to Lufthansa German Airlines and there opened a new phase in his selfless service to humanity.

Bernard Senaya transited to being known as Uncle Sen, the ever diligent, ever helpful Airline Operations staff in one of the world's leading airlines.

His constituency was the Murtala Muhammed International Airport, Lagos and his love permeated every corner of that massive stage where passengers would day-in day-out need a listening ear and a helping hand to be able to either leave or enter our shores. Bernard Senaya, it is reported, was ever so nice and professional in providing top notch services to hundreds of travelers who needed assistance. Even among his colleagues, Uncle Sen was a father figure and an epitome of love and service.

Bernard over the years received his Airline Operators training at Lufthansa, attending several courses locally and internationally and constantly receiving corporate acknowledgements from his employers. Of which he was awarded Employee of the year 2000 (first runner up) As a husband and father, Papa Junior was a gem.

He married his heart throb and mother of their four beautiful children, Josephine (Jossy Joe) in 1977 and together they built a family of their dreams over the years. At home, Papa Junior found it difficult dropping his natural qualities. Home was his training ground for humility, diligence, and love. Bernard was a devout Christian. His strong catholic faith remained steadfast and unwavering until his death.

His church community at CKC Army Dog Centre remained his main focus in his latter days where he served as the Treasurer Parish Pastoral Council (PPC), Vice-Chairman Catholic Men Organization (CMO), Chairman CKC Angelic Choir and chorister and was given recently celebrated as Life Patron of Armed Forces Catholic Choir Association of Nigeria (AFCCAN) He also was also named Patron of the Angelic Choir and given an Award of Honor by the Armed Forces Catholic Chaplaincy.

His immediate community where he lived at Ajasa Command, Ipaja, also enjoyed a huge chunk of his wisdom, kindness, and humility. Bernard Senaya was Chairman of the Residents Association from 2007 to 2011 and remained a key player in the affairs of the community until his passing. In 2020, Bernard Senaya was given an Award of Recognition by the Residents Association for his active participation in the development of his community Bernard Senaya served as President James Adote Akwe Descendants Union (JAADU) for many years steering the family's affairs most diligently until his demise.

Bernard enjoyed reminiscing on his days as a schoolboy soccer maestro, singing soccer war songs and relishing the pain he inflicted on opposing teams in his days. Apart from his love and passion for soccer, he loved to sing and drive. He will be buried wearing his school blazer and tie with a football by his casket. That, no doubt would keep his toothy smiles going till we meet again at Jesus' feet.

Rest on Bernard Kwaku Senaya; Rest peacefully in the bosom of the Lord.

APPENDIX B

AUTHOR'S TRIBUTE TO BERNARD SENAYA

It was with extreme shock and sadness that I received the depressing news of the passing of Bernard Senaya. He was lined up (à la football line up) to provide personal testimonial for the book I am currently writing that is entitled "Tribute to the Great Soccer Players of Saint Finbarr's College." We met in person during Finbarr's North America Reunion in Dayton, Ohio, USA in August 2019. I was on the cusp of contacting him for a scheduled one-on-one interview for the book when the sad news arrived. Without the envisioned personal interview, the book will now consist of only the second-hand stories and testimonies provided by other people (his family, professional colleagues, classmates, and teammates). To commemorate Bernard's attendance at the 2019 SFCOBA North America Reunion, I shared the photo gallery tribute echoed below immediately the sad news was broadcasted on WhatsApp on December 5th, 2022.

Bernard was a resolute and proud wearer of Finbarr's label pin. Once he received his pin, he frequently wore it at many of his public appearances. Many of his photos in years preceding his death showed him in his famous Finbarr's school blazer with the lapel pin affixed on his left-side lapel. He served all and sundry well throughout his illustrious and industrious life. May his gentle soul rest in perfect peace.

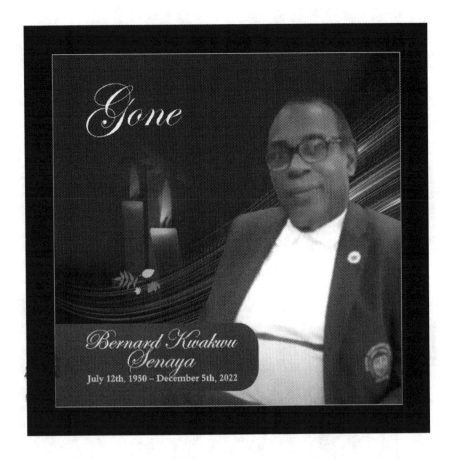

Gone

Bernard Kwakwu
Senaya
July 12th, 1950 – December 5th, 2022

APPENDIX C

JOE IGBOKWE'S TRIBUTE TO FATHER SLATTERY AND SAINT FINBARR'S COLLEGE

Note: Joe Igbokwe, a renowned social author in Lagos, Nigeria, contributed the material in this Appendix to one of my previous Finbarr's books. The contribution is still apt pertinent to the present book on tributes to Finbarr's soccer greats. It is not by coincidence that Igbokwe's writeup is at the intersection of social responsibility and educational commitment, which aligns with Finbarr's theme of Academics, Discipline, and Soccer.

===

Social and Education Commentary
By
Joe Igbokwe

I am told that there are no accidental great men. All great men made themselves in their own image. That which they become, they first desired. The world is divided into people who do things and people who talk about doing things. People who do things have the capacity to inspire and mobilize the masses of the people. The world has found out that it takes good leaders to have a good society, good government, good schools, etc. Leadership is more than just ability.

It is a combination of courage, determination, commitment, character, and ability that makes people willing to follow a leader. Every great leader has left in other people behind him an enduring legacy to hold on to and a vision to continue with.

I read from a school of thought that we are evaluated and classified by four things: what we do, how we look, what we say, and how we say it. A well-known historian, philosopher, H.G. Wells says "the true test of man's greatness is judged by two fundamental questions:

What did he leave to grow?

Did he start men thinking along fresh lines with a vigor that persisted after him?"

People have authored books asking for the Rights of Man, and others have countered the books asking man to seek to earn his rights. According to the latter, we must begin with the charter of duties of man and there is a firm promise that the rights will follow as spring follows the winter. The lesson is that power goes with responsibility and that if we reconcile power with service we are surely on our way to a higher standard of leadership.

A good man, and one of the finest Nigerians in diaspora, the main author of this book, a family friend, Head of Industrial Engineering Department, The University of Tennessee, USA, Prof. Adedeji Badiru, asked me to contribute a chapter to this book from my National Vision perspective. I accepted the offer and went to work. In a letter dated Friday, June 18th, 2004, the Professor gave me the picture of the man called Rev. Father Dennis Slattery. Let me take the liberty of quoting Professor Badiru.

"As you may know, Father Slattery had extensive involvement in the early politics leading to Nigeria's independence, sports, newspaper publication and most notably, education. Apart from being a Roman Catholic Priest, he played many roles in Nigeria. He was an activist for Nigeria's independence. He was a soccer coach and referee. He was a newspaper publisher and editor. He was a teacher, principal and served the government of Nigeria in many advisory roles in education and social issues. He was most widely known for his educational work at St. Finbarr's College, my alma mater. I am one of the prime beneficiaries of his contributions to educational establishments in Nigeria. This, I see as a blessing. Hence the choice of the title: Blessings of a Father. This has both a spiritual connotation as well as a literal interpretation. That I am where I am today is a credit to these blessings brought by the opportunity to attend St. Finbarr's College under Father Slattery's tutelage."

I was also privileged to read the first draft and the updated and edited draft of this book before going to work. I read everything I could find on Father Slattery - everything about him from newspaper columns, magazines, his autobiography, MY LIFE STORY. I asked people who knew him and had personal contact with him to educate me more. In the cause of my findings, I came across a man who was in a hurry to give leadership direction, motivation, inspiration, and momentum. I read about his mission and vision in founding St. Finbarr's College. His national achievements and contributions to project Nigeria from 1944 to 2003 when he died and his famous four commandments of St. Finbarr's College, highlighted the Rev. Father as a great man with an infinite capacity to achieve results.

I came across his views on Nigerian politics, his views on bribery and corruption, his secrets of success and his shrewd antics to get the attention of his students. In this write-up, I will discuss some of the great attributes of this Irish-Nigerian and this foremost educationist called the Enyioha I of Oru, Ahiazu Mbaise and the Oosi Olokun Ijio of Ile-Ife, why he founded St. Finbarr's College, his vision for Nigeria, etc. What was his suggestion on how to restructure Nigeria? What did he say about bribery and corruption, secrets of success and other matters of national significance? What will Nigeria do now to make sure the dreams of late Father Slattery do not fritter away?

FATHER SLATTERY, THE EDUCATIONIST

As one of the frontline nationalists who gave good account of themselves during the struggle for independence, Father Slattery, a man with an eye for the future, had a vision of what the new Nigeria will be like. He knew that when a school is opened the prison gates are closed. He knew that the post-colonial Nigeria would require high-level power that will replace the departing colonial masters. He knew that to get those sound minds would require a sound school. Like the sage called Epictetus, Father Slattery believed that "We must not believe the many, who say that only free people ought to be educated, but we should rather believe the philosophers who say that only the educated are free."

Listen to Rev. Fr. Slattery on why he founded St. Finbarr's College:

"Soon as I recognized that the colonial government was anticipating vast economic and technical changes in the richest of all their colonies - Nigeria. In the immediate future, England saw the necessity of expanded power to meet the anticipated post-war development. It also saw the need to prepare a middle technical power to replace the overseas ex-servicemen who were holding very lucrative posts in the corporations, e.g., the railway, oil companies, industrial development, and so on that could be filled by Nigerian employees at a much

lower scale. Nigerian workers were never paid expatriate allowances, travel allowances, housing allowances or supplied with residences for their families. Without the government informing us, we knew what was needed in this hour of history. There was only one such school planned to meet the demands of the future and it was offered to the Catholic Voluntary Agency. The other agencies felt that they were not qualified to undertake it."

That was how St. Finbarr's College was founded in 1956 and 49 years after, the great school has continued to register its marks in the sands of times. The school has today produced very eminent Nigerian citizens like Professor A. B. Badiru, Admiral Patrick Koshoni, Mr. Tom Borha, Segun Ajanlekoko, Mr Mathias Uzowulu, Nze Mark Odu, Mr. Adesoji Alabi, Dona Oguamanam, R. T. N. Onyeje, Major-Gen. Cyril Iweze, Prof. Steve Elesha, Dr. Francis Ogoegbunam, Mr Chris Uwaje, Mr Jimi Lawal, Coach Steven Keshi, Henry Nwosu, Mr. Benedict Ikwenobe, Mr. Nduka Ugbade, Dr. Segun Ogundimu, Dr. Wole Adedeji, Engr. Festus Orekoya, Senator Adefuye, Mr. Ben Chambang, Mr. Deoye Fajimi, Mr. Adesoji Alabi, Anthony Odugbesan, Engr. Fred Ogundipe, Dr J. A. Ikem, Col. Michael Olusola Akanji, Dr. Omokoya, Dr. John Nwofia, Mr. Philip Bieni, Mr. Sam Cole, and hundreds of others. The mission and the vision of Father Slattery were to join St. Finbarr's with the few existing schools then to produce the high-level manpower that will take over from the colonial masters when they eventually depart. He made a remarkable success out of it.

FATHER SLATTERY AND POLITICS

During the years of the locusts when the military dictator, the late General Sani Abacha, was terrorizing the entire political landscape, Father Slattery, in 1996 made especially useful suggestions that are still relevant to today date. He wrote in his autobiography, *My Life Story*:

What is my recipe for healing the wounds of twenty-six years of military rule and mere ten years of civilian rule? Here is my humble reply:

Thirty years ago, before the fragmentation of this promising country began, I suggested that there should be no more than about eight regions, stop multiplication of states that are eating the national riches of the country, the oil wealth and preventing economic investment to bring employment to the masses.

Turn the present thirty states and Abuja into eight regions and reorganize the district councils into local governments.

We just cannot afford the luxury of thirty state governments, thirty state parliaments, hundreds of commissioners, and thousands of highly paid legislators. We are exploiting the God-given wealth of this country to enrich the rich and starve the poor.

Elect a strong central government and on merit.

Make military coups reasonable and punishable by long-term jail sentences. Confiscate all ill-gotten wealth.

Father Slattery authored this book in 1996 and the Army left in 1999, leaving behind a battered, damaged, looted, disunited and disjointed nation. At the time of writing this, some 400 wise men and women were putting heads together at the on-going National Political Reform Conference to re-design, reconstruct, reposition and re-invent Nigeria to meet the challenges of the 21st century. Nigeria is over-governed with about 801 governments in place. Government officials, their families, cronies, associates, hangers-on, who are not more than 5% of the nation's population, control 80 percent of the nation's resources. Pareto Law allows 20 percent of the population to control 80 percent of the resources. While the greater majority is wallowing in abject poverty, a few sits on the nation's wealth. Now, if we agree that Nigeria is not a rich country which is true, we need to cut our coats according to the size of our cloth. We urgently need to reduce our expenditure in the business of governance.

If you are running a factory and you are not making a profit, you need to look at your entire process.

Are there some workers who are not contributing to the company's profit, and you have no courage to sack them?

Do the workers need re-training?

Are you selling goods to enable you to pay your workers and make reasonable profit for your efforts?

I believe government should operate like a business. If the delegates can muster the courage to listen to Father Slattery and deal squarely with the fraudulent structures that have wasted the scarce resources of this country for years now, we shall be better for it. If the delegates can tackle all the issues disturbing the peace of this nation with manly confidence and brutal frankness, Father Slattery, who worked tirelessly to get this country to work, will continue to rest in peace.

HIS MANY WORRIES ON CORRUPTION

Another big problem that kept Father Slattery awake at night in Nigeria was the issue of bribery and corruption. Shortly before he died, the Rev. Father screamed to anybody who cared to listen, "Look at Nigeria today, several years after independence. Today, sad to say, Nigeria is riddled with corruption from the top to the bottom. No segment of Nigerian society is free from the cankerworm of bribery that has eaten into the bowels of our nation."

President Obasanjo saw the rot and devastation that the scourge had brought to the nation when he came to power in 1999 and promised that it was not going to be business as usual. The late Senate President, Chief Chuba Okadigbo had to be impeached for corruption. In 2003 some prominent Nigerians were summoned for helping themselves to the public till to the tune of almost two billion naira, being part of the money meant for the 27-year-old National Identity Card project. The accused include former ministers, a serving minister, and other prominent citizens. They are Hussaini Akwanga, minister for Labor and Productivity and former Permanent Secretary in the Ministry of Internal Affairs, late Sunday Afolabi, former Minister for Internal Affairs, and Okwesilieze Nwodo, former secretary of the ruling People's Democratic Party (PDP). Others are Mohammed Shata, former minister of state for Internal Affairs Ministry, Tumi Mohammed, former Director, Department of Civic Registration (DCR), Niyi Adelakun, former representative of SAGEM SA, and Christopher Agidi.

Akwanga's successor, Mrs. R. O. Akerele was later arrested, and she was reported to have admitted receiving $500,000 in bribery. A former Inspector General of Police, Mr. Tafa Balogun, had to be sacked for corruption and he is now facing a 70-count charge. Recently, a Minister of Education, Professor Fabian Osuji was sacked for corruption. The current President of the Senate, Senator Adolphus Wabara has just been removed as the Senate President, making it the third Senate President to be removed since 1999 for the same offence.

It is disheartening to note here that the National Assembly has become the greatest obstacle in the fight against corruption in Nigeria since 1999.

It was the late Chief Bola Ige of the blessed memory that first gave me a hint on the type of people we have in the National Assembly. Bola Ige told me, "Joe, you need to know the kind of people we have in the National Assembly. You need to see their demands. You should fight to go to the National Assembly in 2003. This nation must be saved."

When I was told then that large sums of money had to be paid out by the Ministries to get their budgets approved, I never believed it. When I was told that even the presidency would have to part with millions to get the national budget to sail through, I never believed too. When Mallam El-Rufai raised an alarm that Alhaji Mantu and Senator Jonathan Zwingina demanded N54m to endorse him as a minister, they denied it. When Hon. Yerima accused the National Assembly members of taking recharge cards from GSM companies, he was promptly suspended for one month. Stories have been told of how the National Assembly paid the national budget with billions of naira to have enough money to take care of themselves before the budget is allowed to sail through.

Professor Soludo's mandate to banks to raise their capital base to N25b in 2004 has been sabotaged by the National Assembly. After collecting huge sums of money from the banks, they now divided the banks into three categories: N5b, N10b, and N25b. I know a member of the House of Representatives from one of the zones in the South that has purchased about six houses in Abuja and other places within two years of sojourn in the House.

Nigerians also remember that the former Senate President, Chief Adolphus Wabara, pleaded for the understanding of National Assembly members because, according to him, "they are trying to recoup the money they spent during the elections." Governors in the South cart away something close to N30b of federal allocations every month and yet a visit to the zone shows little development. A Minister of State in the Ministry of Finance,

Mrs. Nenadi Usman once alerted the nation that our governors and local government chairs are siphoning the people's money outside the country. According to her, once the monthly allocation is released, the value of foreign currencies goes up.

It is not enough for us to plead with our creditors for debt relief, we must show that we are serious people. Our governors and local government chairs cannot continue to stash away billions of dollars in foreign accounts while we are asking for debt relief. Officials of the World Bank, International Finance Corporation and the Paris Club are aware of these foreign accounts and will laugh their heads off any time such a request is made.

There are other cases which time and space will not permit me to mention here. However, the truth remains that corruption has become the biggest problem facing the nation. The states and local governments are still wallowing in deep corruption. It has stunted our growth for years. Money meant for development has ended up in private accounts and Father Slattery saw it and raised an alarm. The late Professor Bade Onimade said, "It has been estimated that between 1973 and 1995, Nigeria earned about five times the total amount of money that went into the US Marshal Plan for the reconstruction of Western Europe after World War II, yet Nigeria is crying for reconstruction 23 years after all that money." I make bold to suggest that the fight against corruption must be a collective responsibility. I enjoin well-meaning Nigerians to rise in support of the president to deal with this hydra-headed monster to free the funds needed for development. This is a task that must be done.

FATHER SLATTERY'S SECRETS OF SUCCESS

In this season where many able-bodied Nigerians are looking for short cuts to success, Rev. Father Slattery warned that wealth is created by going under the engines where hands are made dirty. According to Father

Slattery, "There is no secret about success. I do believe that success lies in acknowledging one's limitations and applying one's talent very well to whatever one is doing. Success, in my view, is about 80 percent sweat and 20 percent talent. Sometimes, geniuses fail because they cannot work hard while people of lesser talent succeed because they are diligent. Nobody will ever die of challenging work. A lot of people die of laziness, doing nothing and growing fat.

This is a lesson for those who want to pass exams without reading, those who want wealth without work, those who want to live in the best houses in town, drive the best cars and wear expensive clothes without knowing how to make a kobo through dint of hard work, those who waste away their youths only to become beggars at old age, and those who waste the precious gift of time on frivolities like 419 and what have you. Those who had the privilege of traveling to places like the United States, Germany, Japan, South Korea, and few other places in Europe have acknowledged the obvious and painful fact that Nigerians are not working hard enough to build their country. Everybody wants to be an importer of foreign goods and yet we want our economy to grow. We want our currency to stabilize. We want jobs for our children and yet we do things that will jeopardize our economy. We want to be like Japan, USA, France, etc. but we do not want to pay the price. We do not want to do what they did to become what they are today. Building a nation is not a tea party. It requires commitment and serious-minded leaders and followers.

SLATTERY'S ANTICS TO MAKE STUDENTS PAY ATTENTION

Father Slattery was also known for what Professor Badiru called "shrewd antics" to get the attention of his students. I enjoin readers to read in this book the account of Professor Badiru himself in a sub-title he called the Immaculate Conception Question. It is a must read for teachers in our primary and secondary schools. It is a teaching technique that will empower the students to strive for excellence. My father employed similar antics on his children when we were young. Once you came home with your results, my father would go straight to your scores in English and Mathematics. If you failed in both subjects my father would tell you at once that you were not in school.

It made most of his children excel in English and Mathematics. My penchant for mathematics and eventual training in Mechanical Engineering had its roots in my father's antics. I know a man who went to Navy School, Abeokuta to pick his son for holidays only to discover to his chagrin that the boy performed so badly in the examination. Out of annoyance, coupled with the powerful desire to make the boy know that he was not happy with his result, the man left his son in school for three days when other students had gone home for holidays. That singular attitude of the father changed the son's life forever, as the boy later became one of the best students in that school.

I have heard stories of parents who are always in the habit of telling you how long their daughters' hair is and how beautiful they look. They will also tell you how handsome their boys are. The same parents will care less if their children do not know how to conjugate verbs. The same parents will not sit down to teach their children how to juggle variables to achieve results or solve simple mathematical problems. A basic knowledge of Mathematics helps to build logical thinking. Without a logical thinking ability, children can quickly go astray. Parents should pay less attention to vanity and more attention to preparing their children for the challenges of life that they will face later. The power of a person is based on how well he or she uses his or her intrinsic intelligence.

CONCLUSION

The Irish-Nigerian Father Slattery came to Nigeria in 1941 as a Catholic Priest, founded St. Finbarr's College in 1956 and trained hundreds of minds. He played politics, managed football, managed a newspaper and conducted other wonderful projects too numerous to mention here. Dale Carnegie once wrote that there is an old saying he had cut out and pasted on his mirror where he could not help but see it every day: "I shall pass this way but once; any good, therefore, that I can do or any kindness that I can show to any human being, let me do it now. Let me not defer nor neglect it for I shall not pass this way again."

I can say at once without fear of contradiction that Rev. Father Slattery read the old saying and insisted on putting it to practice in Nigeria. A thousand years will pass, and Nigerians will ever continue to take notice of the fact that a Father Slattery once passed this way and left an indelible mark in the sands of time. His clever work in Nigeria will stand the test of time. To die completely is to be forgotten. When a person is not forgotten, he has not died. Father Slattery lives on. His enduring legacies live on. His vision for Nigeria and the Black man lives on.

INFORMATION SOURCES

Slattery, Denis J., My Life Story, West African Book Publishers Limited, Ilupeju, Lagos, Nigeria, 1996.

Official Commissioning of PTA Projects: Programme of Events, St. Finbarr's College, Akoka, December 16, 2004.

The Finbarrian: Official Newsletter of Saint Finbarr's College Old Boys' Association, Vol. 8, Jan. 1999.

APPENDIX D

SOCCER SONGS OF SAINT FINBARR'S COLLEGE

Begin Warm Up: (Before start of any song)
Lead: Esobe Zangaruwa
Response: Yeah!
(2ce)

1) GRAND OLD TEAM

We've a grand old team to play for us
Tralalala la la la la. Tra la la la la la
When you read the history, Pam Pam (bang your feet or clap 2ce)
It's enough to cause your heart cheer er er
For we don't care whether we win or lose or draw
The warriors be stared
For we always know there is going to be a match and St Finbarr's
College must be there
Must be there
Finbarr's, Finbarr's
Finbarr's Finbarr's Finbarr's
F I N B A R R ' S - FINBARR'SSSSS!!!!

2) WE PLAY AT TIMES

Lead: We play at times

Response: We play at times

Lead: And race and run

Response: And race and run

Lead: I'll tell you why

Response: I'll tell you why

Lead: For love of game

Response: For love of game

All: Ha ha ha play you Finbarr's play you game

All: Ha ha ha play you Finbarr's play you game for love of game

All: Ha ha ha play you Finbarr's play you game, for fun for love of game

Up School, Up FINBARR'S !!!!!

3) WHEN I WENT TO FINBARR'S

When I went to Finbarr's

What did I see

The Akoka boys were playing with Supreme as their coach

HOLY, singing Hallelujah

Singing Hallelujah, singing Hallelujah, Holy

HOLY, singing Hallelujah

Singing Hallelujah, singing Hallelujah, Holy!!!

4) ZINGA ZINGA BOM BOM

Lead: St Finbarr's

Response: Zinga Zinga Bom Bom, Zinga Zinga

Lead: St Finbarrrrrrr's

Response: Zinga Zinga Bom Bom, Zinga Zinga

Lead: En goyama goyama

Response: Ya Bom, Ya Bom, Ya bom, Iya Bom.

5) OUR COLOURS

Lead: Our Colours

Response: Blue Yellow Blue

Lead: Our colleagues

Response: Up Finbarr's

All: We shall never, never, never, never lose this match (2ce)

All: We shall never, never, never, never lose this YEAR! Up Finbarr's!

6) OWEGBELUGBO

Lead: Owegbelugbo o

Response: St Finbarr's

Lead: Owegbelugbo

Response: St Finbarr's

Lead: Owegbelugbo o

Response: St Finbarr's

Lead: Owegbelugbo

Response: St Finbarr's

All: Ade o ri wa o

Response: St Finbarr's

All: Owegbelugbo

Response: St Finbarr's

All: Bata ese wa o

Response: St Finbarr's

All: Owegbelugbo o

Lead: Ama nor Igbobi

All: St Finbarr's

Lead: Ama nor St Gregory's

All: St Finbarr's

7) HOLY HOLY (Victory Song)

Holy, holy- Holy, holy! Holy, holy!

St Finbarr's Akoka, another champion

HOLY HOLY (Victory Song)

Holy, holy- Holy, holy! Holy, holy!

St Finbarr's Akoka, another champion

I begi teach them soccer

Oh, oh, oh, oh, oh - oh, oh, oh, oh - oh, oh, oh oh!

I begi show them soccer

Oh, oh, oh, oh, oh - oh, oh, oh, oh - oh, oh, oh oh!

8) WADELE

Lead: Wa de le oh, wa de le oh oh

All: Wa de, wadele oh oh

Lead: Father Slattery eiye wa de le oh oh

All: Wa de, wadele oh oh

Lead: (captain's name, players names) wa de le oh oh

All: Wa de, wadele oh oh

All: Wa de le oh, wa de le oh oh

All: Wa de, wadele oh oh

All: Wa de leeeee wa de le oh (2ce)

9) FINBARRS BOYS ARE THERE AGAIN

Lead: Finbarr's boys are there again

All: Hallelujah

Lead: To teach them to play soccer

All: Hallelujah

Lead: (Captain's name) is there today

All: Hallelujah

(Charged Version for when the players start scoring goals)
All: Finbarr's Boys have come again oh oh to teach them how to play soccer!!!
Finbarr's Boys oh oh
Have come again
To teach them how to play soccer

10) IF YOU GO TO BRAZIL
Lead: If you go to Brazil and bring Sir Pele
All: Finbarr's are winning today
All: Finbarr's are winning, Finbarr's are winning
All: Finbarr's are winning TODAY!!!

11) MERRY MERRY ST FINBARR'S
Merry merry St Finbarr's oh oh
Merry merry St Finbarr's
Ah ah - Ah ah
Merry merry St Finbarr's
Merry merry Father Slattery oh oh
Merry merry Father Slattery
Ah ah - ah ah
Merry merry Father Slattery
(Players names also)

12) PRAYER HYMN (HOLY QUEEN)
Holy Queen we bend before Thee
Queen of purity divine
Make us love Thee we implore Thee
Make us truly to be thine
CHORUS
Teach us teach
Teach us teach us Holy Mother

How to conquer every sin
How to love
How to love and help each other
At the prize of life to win

Unto Thee a child was given
Greater than the son of men
Coming down from highest heaven
To create the world again

Chorus - Teach us teach us

13) The proud big boys, they conquered many schools
But when they meet St Finbarrs
We shall throw them to the window
The window, the window the
window, window, window

UP SCHOOL !!!! UP F I N B A R R ' S !!!!!!!!

<u>VERSE 1</u>
SAINT FINBARR'S COLLEGE AKOKA
MY OWN ALMA MATA
I'M PROUD TO BELONG
I'M PROUD TO BELONG
TO THE CITADEL OF EXCELLENCE

Chorus:
FIDELITAS…
FIDE-DE-LITAS
FIDELITAS…
FIDE-DE-LITAS
FIDELITAS

VERSE 2

JOY AND HAPPINESS IS OURS
WHENEVER WE REMEMBER YOU
A PLACE EVERYONE x2
IS LOVED AND CARED FOR OOOO

Chorus:
FIDELITAS...
FIDE-DE-LITAS
FIDELITAS...
FIDE-DE-LITAS
FIDELITAS

Courtesy of 2019 SFCOBA-America Reunion, Dayton, Ohio, USA, August 16-18, 2019

(Sponsored, Prepared, and Printed by ABICS Publications, www. abicspublications.com)

Printed in the United States
by Baker & Taylor Publisher Services